ENGAGING MILLENNIAL FACULTY

Michael G. Strawser
Russell Carpenter

NEW FORUMS

NEW FORUMS PRESS INC.

Published in the United States of America
by New Forums Press, Inc.1018 S. Lewis St.
Stillwater, OK 74074
www.newforums.com

Copyright © 2019 by New Forums Press, Inc.

Library of Congress Cataloging-in-Publication Data Pending

This book may be ordered in bulk quantities at discount from New Forums Press, Inc., P.O. Box 876, Stillwater, OK 74076 [Federal I.D. No. 73 1123239]. Printed in the United States of America.

ISBN 10: 1-58107-339-9
ISBN 13: 978-1-58107-339-3

Table of Contents

Introduction

I (Michael) need to be careful, as I tend to rebel against volumes that generalize or provide broad based claims. I also tend to rebel against volumes with minimal citations. Unfortunately, I, along with Russell Carpenter, wrote a volume that: a) makes generalized broad-based claims and b) uses citations sporadically. Ugh. Here's the deal…

I love researching generational differences. I believe generational differences have the potential to become too generalized (and therefore not helpful) but, as a platform for discussing workplace effectiveness and workplace differences, generational differences help provide context. Unfortunately, generational differences in higher education can be a difficult subject to explore. For instance, there is a broad spectrum represented by generations in higher ed. Comparatively, the retirement age of faculty is older than the traditional workplace and the starting age of new faculty is older as well because of the time it takes to complete degree requirements. This creates a unique environment.

It is important though, especially as we start to see a wave of millennial faculty, that we appropriately address how faculty demographics will change and how that will impact the higher education environment at large. For purposes of this volume, we need to think strategically about how we *engage* millennial faculty in what has been a typically anti-millennial infrastructure. So, I would ask that you be patient with this volume. It has been developed as a practical resource. Pause as you fume at generalized generational differences and remember that not everyone fits into one box: every millennial is different, every boomer is different, etc. Still, we hope this volume will be helpful, no matter your feelings on generational differences, as you look to serve and support all faculty.

Michael G. Strawser
Assistant Professor, Communication
University of Central Florida

Section I
Maximizing Millennial Talent in Higher Education

There was nothing new under the sun—and then came millennials. There have certainly been countless volumes written about how millennials have changed … everything. However, we are still seeing the initial repercussions of millennials in workplace environments and as participants in organizational structures.

Millennials

Who are millennials? Typically, millennials are defined as those born between 1980-1996 (although this range is debated). Unfortunately they have a reputation for being lazy, entitled, and high maintenance; yet, they are also highly networked, appreciate life experiences, and are tech-savvy (Morreale & Staley, 2016). Despite obvious difficulties *generalizing* traits and characteristics, the generation presents a fascinating and necessary area of focus.

Think about it…

As you think about "millennials," what stereotypes or pre-conceptions do you have about this generation?

_____

_____

_____

_____

_____

One particularly mesmerizing professional realm that will have long-term millennial repercussions is higher education. As millennial employees (both faculty and staff) contribute to higher education institutions, they should be willing and able to respond to current practices; however, institutions may also need to adapt to this new generation.

Because millennials are just now fully immersed in the higher education culture as faculty and staff, rather than as students, the ramifications of how institutions will navigate them have yet to be fully understood. We do know that millennials will challenge the status quo: they do not go quietly into the night and often refuse the answer "because that is how it has always been done…" and, as such, they may refuse to accept tradition as a valid excuse for present behavior. Some may lament this distinction, but, because of their background and upbringing, millennials must be uniquely approached and engaged in all professional contexts, especially postsecondary education.

Think about it...

How have you observed the millennial impact on the workforce?

_____

_____

_____

_____

_____

How have you observed the millennial impact on postsecondary education?

_____

_____

_____

_____

_____

Despite differences in specifying a date range for millennials, the year 2013, or even more generally the 2010-2015 window, represents the first wave of millennial faculty. Onboarding and developing this new generation requires intentional planning regarding institutional technology use, faculty recruitment and development, as well as collaborative work and decision making (Kelly, 2009). Traditionally, millennials want flexibility, collaboration, and constant communication, particularly about results and achievement. These characteristics could have a positive influence on faculty, yet the actual integration of millennials into the higher education environment has invited complex questions. And, to complicate matters, millennials must engage with a new generation (Z) of students. Gen Z students, while similar to millennials in some respects, are still unique themselves.

If the attempt to retain and develop millennial faculty is not a university-wide directive, then institutional challenges will persist. To address millennial faculty concerns, especially in the classroom, faculty and educational developers should establish programs that engage, inspire and transform millennial faculty. Since millennials "changed" education as students, how should faculty support systems and faculty development programs adapt to meet the needs of this new faculty population?

Think about it...

Would you agree that millennials have changed "education" in general? Why or why not? If so, how have they changed higher education?

_____

_____

_____

_____

_____

_____

A Generation Comparison

What is a generation? Typically, "a generation" consists of those born within a similar time frame who share life experiences such as pop culture, world events, economic conditions, natural disasters, and technology (Schullery, 2013). Why is a generational understanding important? In the workplace, four generations may work alongside each other: baby boomers (1946-1964), Generation X (1965-1981), millennials (1982-1996) and Generation Z (1997-2012). This section will focus on each generation from several perspectives.

Strauss and Howe (1991) believed the twenty-year age range, broadly, for a generational grouping is appropriate because it allows for consistency in terms of a birth and child-rearing span and it also allows members to go through the four stages of development: youth, rising adult, middle and old age. Each generation has a story and it is important to highlight generational differences and unique traits. A clear understanding of generational differences is important for organizations, especially higher education, as considerations of workforce management, retention and recruitment must be taken into account (Chenovich & Cates, 2016).

Traditionalists

While traditionalists are not currently active in organizations, they have had a significant impact on the modern workplace. It is hard to not "generalize" different generations but, in some ways, we must. It is helpful to position different generations as distinct from previous or future groups. Traditionalists have experienced feast and famine, numerous tragic world events, significant technological innovation, and workforce transitions.

Sons and daughters of "The Greatest Generation", traditionalists are very loyal to *the system,* which impacted how they advanced professionally (and how they left the workplace for future generations). The system, to traditionalists, is primary and a good employee functions within the confines of the system. Typically, for traditionalists, a millennial mindset would be anarchy and disloyal. When they were of age, traditionalists took a job and stayed in that job for decades. Hard times were followed by prosperity and this group consisted of foundational rule-followers. They put their head down, toed the company line, and made a life for themselves within the confines of the workplace infrastructure. They were conformists, hard-working and loyal employees.

If traditionalists have retired and are not currently engaged in corporations, why is it important to still recognize their generational contribution? What many may not consider is the impact of traditionalists on: a) higher education today and b) the resistance to the millennial faculty mindset. "Traditionalists" followed the rules and, in many ways, the millennial mindset is counter to that mentality. The lasting legacy of traditionalists is a concrete and foundational corporate infrastructure that still influences boomer-leaders. This impacts communication, innovation and the status quo.

Think about it…

In your interactions with "Traditionalists", how have they exemplified the description above?

_____

_____

_____

_____

_____

_____

Baby Boomers

The boomers have been referred to by some as the "Me" generation. They are activists, radicals, and "anti" (at least growing up) traditional patterns and trends. Boomers, for the most part, are leaders in organizations. Similar to traditionalists, boomers are career-loyalists. They are also professionally competitive, *very* career focused and tend to hesitate when it comes to "trusting" Gen X, Gen Y (millennials), and Gen Z. This generation holds a significant position of power in corporate-America today, but 80 million boomers will leave the workforce within the next decade. Even though boomer faculty members and administrators are staying longer, they will eventually leave higher education in waves, or, more accurately, a tsunami.

Baby boomers, those who rejected traditional cultural norms, went on to become a wealthy consumer base. Boomers, who earned their name from a boom in birth rates following WWII, value financial prosperity. During this generational shift, women also entered the workforce in unprecedented numbers, which dramatically influenced family roles.

Within organizations, baby boomers are classified as career loyalists, believing that job-hopping negatively affects career advancement. This sentiment may be bristled at by millennials. Boomers are "workaholics," committed to long work hours, and stressed due to little leisure time (again—anti-millennial). Many boomers have stayed in their organizations longer than anticipated, primarily because of the 2008-recession but also because they enjoy work. Because of this delay, Generation X members may miss out on key leadership positions as millennials enter the workforce in droves and "come to power". Boomers established a workplace precedent-minimal flexibility, loyal to "the job" and/ or organization, top-down structures and long-hours. Many of these characteristics run counter to what millennials care about. Boomers are, in sum, career loyalists, professionally competitive and are often labeled as workaholics.

Think about it…

In your interactions with "boomers", how have they exemplified the description above?

_____

_____

_____

_____

_____

_____

_____

Generation X

When experts mention generations in the workplace, Gen X is often forgotten, and, in some ways, for good reason. By sheer numbers Gen X (51 million) is much smaller than boomers (80 million) and millennials (75 million). Xers, born between 1965-1980, are small but mighty. Generally, Gen X values balance, independence, autonomy, pragmatism and self-reliance. They are also cynical and skeptical. They grew up having to take care of themselves, as their parents invented the 60-hour work week, which impacted their perceptions. Xers are more anti-establishment than the boomers and are primarily results-oriented. Gen X values work/life balance, more so than their boomer parents, and their work is less tied to their identity. "Work smarter, not harder" has established an internal desire for output, yet the struggle to respect (and trust) authority remains. Xers want efficiency in the workplace, access to leaders and information, and they want to know *why* they are completing a task or a job.

Gen X, independent and autonomous, are cynical but brought forth an entrepreneurial spirit and trailblazed new technological developments. This tech-savvy generation, in many ways, became a bridge to those segments of the population now coined millennials and Generation Z. After Gen X, the world would not be the same. Rapid innovations, such as social media, the birth of mobile phones, and eventually wearable technologies established a new way of thinking, and acting. Gen X members, in summary, are rebellious, were part of the protest movement, are a little cynical and mistrusting, less motivated by money, and appreciate/desire a strong work-life balance.

Think about it…

In your interactions with "Gen X", how have they exemplified the description above?

_____

_____

_____

_____

_____

_____

_____

_____

Generation Z

Members of Generation Z are entrepreneurial, insanely tech-savvy and collaborative. Pew Research Center designated 1997 as the first year of the "post-millennials" and while many refer to this Generation as "Gen Z", an official name has yet to be decided. No matter how you label them, however, Gen Z is "different" from millennials.

While this is a volume on millennial faculty, it is important to remember that millennial faculty began their higher ed careers engaging with Gen Z students. Practically this means they have probably been influenced by the desires of this student population and while faculty and student desires are not always at-odds, there can be conflicting outcomes or end goals.

The verdict is still out on some Gen Z traits, as many members of this generation are still exploring their formative years, but we know their parents are typically members of Gen X or Gen Y (i.e. millennials), they tend to be risk averse, entrepreneurial and image-driven. In the classroom they want experiential learning and they have a strong connection to their values and social causes.

Think about it…

In your interactions with "Gen Z", how have they exemplified the description above?

_____

_____

_____

_____

_____

_____

_____

_____

Millennials and Millennial Faculty

Leading millennial faculty may require, in many ways, a new way of thinking. Thankfully, universities can research millennial characteristics to understand how this new wave of faculty members may interact with their students, peers and the institution at large. The following section describes millennials, and millennial faculty characteristics through four categorical lenses: expectations; work; authority; and relationships.

Expectations

Millennials are accustomed to systems adapting to "them"—not the other way around. As students, at all education levels, millennials traditionally clamored for something different. Broadly, and maybe most importantly, it is important to recognize that millennials value and strive for perfectionism. Mukherjee (2018) describes perfectionism as: "intense personal and external drives to thrive under certain societal metrics, potentially by placing far too much pressure and excessive expectations on one's self" (para. 2). A study, released in 2017 by Curran and Hill, revealed that societal perfectionism is increasing over time. This perfectionism drive is due, in part, to millennials. While a perfectionist mentality sounds positive, Curran and Hill (2017) remind their readers that perfectionism can be damaging and unhealthy.

For millennials, the drive and desire to be perfect creates an unrealistic expectation for themselves and others. This desire has professional implications, which will be discussed later, but it also has implications in other areas as well.

Unrealistic expectations, in some ways, define Generation

Y. Millennials have created a world where instant gratification rules the day. This can manifest itself in the desire for material possessions as well as professional status and work. This means some millennials may want what their parents have accumulated over decades, yet millennials want it earlier.

Generally, opinions regarding millennials range from devastating to unhelpful; yet, it is important to wrestle with the millennial mentality. For some members of Gen Y, good enough is not really good enough and average is unacceptable. This mentality manifests itself in several ways, but it is important to at least understand that millennials approach work as they do life: with expectations that are far-reaching and may be unmet or unfulfilled.

As a result, institutions must deal with unrealistic expectations. Faculty developers, administrators, faculty and staff have experience working through millennial desires—millennials were once students, after all. Yet student concerns vary greatly from those of a working professional and the life stage of a student is fleeting, seasonal. Most people have 12-16 years in school before they start their professional careers. The time one devotes to student life pales in comparison to professional existence. Institutions, then, must learn to function and thrive as employees grapple with unrealistic expectations of themselves and others.

Millennial faculty are not immune to expectations in the workplace or in their personal lives. While faculty developers and administrators should consider the role of expectations, perfectionism has the potential to be most damaging. Higher education presents inordinate opportunities for imperfect products. Journal submissions are rejected, initiatives are rebuffed, student evaluations are negative, etc. The higher ed environment is not unique, as other professional contexts deal with expectations, but colleges and universities build faculty job descriptions on the basis of subjective feedback. At the very least it is important to help faculty deal with their expectation perceptions and create a climate of realistic support.

How does your institution perpetuate millennial expectations?

_____

_____

_____

_____

_____

How can your university engage millennial faculty expectations without succumbing to a complete culture or climate overhaul?

_____

_____

_____

_____

_____

Work

One problem with millennial-specific (or generation-specific) resources is the reality that all members of a particular generation are not the same. Curating one definition of a generation can be damaging because it allows for generalizations and may create inaccuracies. Yet there are similarities and differences amongst those who share generational distinctions. Because there are similarities it can be helpful to think about how to engage a generation holistically.

An accurate understanding of expectations can help university administrators interact with, and think about, millennials. The expectations, especially perfectionism, discussed in the previous section can serve as platform that helps employers and university administrators think about interacting with and engaging millennials. There are, however, distinctive work-based realities that tend to be more "millennial-friendly".

Let's start with the positive. Millennials enjoy collaboration, group work and shared responsibility. If your institution develops effective systems, this can allow for innovation and cross-generational teamwork. Unfortunately, the millennial concept of shared responsibility may lead some to forgo or decide not to pursue leadership positions. Despite their reluctance to lead in certain situations, millennials want to engage in collaborative teams, and they find teamwork valuable. For millennial workers, teamwork must be efficient, and roles clarified, or it can become a frustrating endeavor. This is not unique to them as all generations though would prefer any teamwork initiatives be strategic and intentional.

Millennials want to be part of the conversation. This team mentality can be hard for Generation X employees and bosses because of their tendency to be more independent and approach work as a solo-force. Boomers may also rebel against the thought that millennials want to be included in important conversations so early in their careers. Like most employees, millennials want to be trusted and have some shared ownership of their work responsibilities.

The overarching perfectionism expectation manifests itself in millennial work desires. For instance, millennials want technology to be used efficiently. Up to date technology systems and platforms are important for Generation Y because there is a recognition that technology can speed up tasks and work in general. The tech-savvy nature of millennials also influences their desire for communication that is electronic and produces a greater level of information exchange and productivity.

Millennials also have different expectations of their work leaders. More so than previous generations, millennials want leaders who are transparent (as millennials grew up in the social and digital age of transparency) and who can communicate a clear and shared vision. Millennials want the 'big picture' of their organization to be front and center. They need to know that their job is purposeful and that they fulfill a necessary role in the larger scheme. As such, the quality of the manager or supervisor, as well as the quality of the management team, continue to be important factors for millennial job seekers.

Millennial-friendly managers should help their employees feel engaged at work. Employee engagement, while not a unique problem for millennials, continues to be a struggle with each new generational workforce shift. Millennial employees want growth opportunities in their vocations and want to know that their manager will meet professional development needs.

Ultimately, and most practically for the purposes of this volume, it is important to think about the impact of these work expectations on faculty members and faculty development. Institutions would be wise to set up a systematic culture of collaboration and interdisciplinary teaching, service and scholarship. The millennial desire for team-based responsibilities and initiatives will serve the university well as disciplinary lines are crossed. It is necessary to consider how these relationships will be fostered and encouraged.

Institutions may also develop new IT and information systems that establish clear (and efficient) lines of communication-beyond the traditional office phone or email message. Project management software or social networks can be utilized on campuses to establish relationships and, again, encourage collaboration.

Finally, administrators and faculty developers should begin to design a strategy for encouraging millennial participation in vision and mission discussions. Millennials want a seat at the table and while they are not entitled to participate it does benefit an institution to encourage shared dialogue when it is appropriate or helpful.

Think about it...

What about your institution would you consider millennial-friendly?

_____

_____

_____

_____

_____

_____

How can your university encourage millennial participation related to big picture organizational questions and issues?

_____

_____

_____

_____

_____

_____

Authority

Millennial perspectives of authority and authoritative figures coincide with their general expectations and work ideals. Prossack (2018) said it this way, and this qualifier can be helpful: "authoritarian leadership is out, and inclusive leadership is in" (para. 1). Naturally, this leads one to assume that millennials are "anti-authority" and in some cases this may be true. But traditionally all generations experience some anti-authority tendencies. The difference for millennials is the expected leadership characteristics that result- meaning, they expect more of their leaders compared to Boomers and Gen X.

Boomers responded to, and became, authoritarian leaders. Granted, this is a generalization, but boomer-leaders would typically demand or command and leave little room for facilitation or communal direction. In many ways boomers built a career trajectory striving to be the leader who was separate from the troops, nestled in the corner office. It is important to note that this type of leadership, more authoritarian and top-down, can be effective. Yet, it is likely to fall on deaf ears when it comes to Generation Y.

Boomers are certainly more hierarchical, especially compared to millennials; yet, in relation to their traditionalist predecessors, boomers actually strive for more consensus regarding organizational decisions. The top-down model where they "grew up" professionally was impressive to boomer employees. Typically, boomers aligned themselves with one organization and stayed there (or are still there) until retirement.

Gen X, on the other hand, is a little more autonomous. They

like to press leaders by challenging and asking "why". Xers will typically make waves and are not as easily impressed. Compared to boomers, Gen X will be more blunt and more direct in terms of communication style while being much less loyal to the organization or the company's mission. Technology is a driving force for this generation, as they love efficiency and balancing work-life, and they will respond to constructive criticism—but not micro-management—not dissimilar to millenials.

Here's the deal. In any organization, higher education included, boomers, Gen X, millennials, and now Gen Z must co-exist. The views of authority discussed above are counter to the traditional millennial understanding of "boss", "manager" or "leader". Millennials want to rid themselves of authoritarian leaders. This means the top-down approach that relies on hierarchy and loyalty to the individual is no longer as effective. Instead, millennials want inclusive, or participative, leaders.

Inclusive and participative leadership structures must incorporate a true team mentality where shared responsibility reigns supreme. As the lines of identity become even more blurry, millennials tend to see work as an extension of their inner-self. This means they want a collegial environment and are more likely to view coworkers as friends. The shared responsibility can impact millennial desires for leadership stature. They, at least right now, may shy away from leadership positions because of the sole-responsibility a leader assumes.

Culture, for millennials, is important. They tend to desire an enjoyable corporate culture that is collaborative, creative, and achievement-oriented. A dark culture of distrust and menial and/or busy work will repulse millennials. They want to know that their leaders are strong, ethical, and transparent. They also need a justification for the work they are doing (i.e. "because I said so" may not work for this group).

Millennials want access to authority figures. They want a seat at the table, and they want to know their opinion was heard, even if it wasn't acted on. The desire for access to high-ranking officials is a noble concept, but millennials have the tendency to take it too far and assume that access and transparency are entitlements. This has the potential to cause derision and combative assumptions.

All told, millennials want authority figures who will listen to their ideas, provide access and feedback, and reiterate the "why" of organizational decisions. These desires, in and of themselves, are not absurd and, in fact, are shared by some members of the baby boomer or Gen X demographic.

Think about it...

Describe the organizational structure of your institution.

_____
_____
_____
_____
_____
_____

Describe the organizational culture of your institution.

_____
_____
_____
_____
_____
_____

If your institution wanted to facilitate a more transparent, open and collaborative climate, what challenges would exist?

_____
_____
_____
_____
_____
_____

Relationships

Expectations, workplace dynamics, and views on authority can all be approached through a millennial lens. The millennial-specific characteristics discussed here resonate across the generational spectrum. Most have either encountered millennial expectations or are living in the midst of millennial ideals. The impact is far-reaching. Yet one of the most intriguing concepts for higher education professionals to consider may be millennial views on relationships in general.

Millennials grew up in a world where 50% of them had divorced parents. While this characteristic may not seem to connect strongly to the workplace, the perception of some millennials may be that relationships are finite. This could impact, negatively, millennial views on company loyalty and entitlement. For example, millennials are leaving jobs more consistently compared to their Gen X predecessors (Alton, 2018). The "what have you done for me lately" model seems alive and well in the millennial psyche.

Additionally, technology, specifically social platforms, has created a world of know and be known. In an article for *The Atlantic*, Jean Twenge (2017) reflects on the immense implications of technology, specifically smart phones. Her observations, while primarily focused on post-millennials, have ramifications for those in the Generation Y cohort. Twenge (2017) mentions the impact of uber-connectedness not only on social interactions but also mental health.

The millennial drive and desire to be known through social platforms, the desire for "likes", "retweets", and opinion-affirmation, could present challenges in an institution, like higher education, that typically engages in (sometimes) reasoned and critical debate between faculty peers, faculty-staff and faculty-administration.

In the workplace, millennials tend to value relationships that cross hierarchical platforms. For instance, their views on their boss, seeing their supervisor in more of a mentor-leader role, will continue to become more complex. Millennials also crave organizational socialization. They want to know how they fit in as a member of the organization and the purpose they serve (Myers & Sadaghiani, 2010). Ultimately, they find great worth and value in their ability to be a vital member of an organization.

Unfortunately, millennial upbringing also impacts their workplace performance, or at least workplace dynamics. especially interactions with peers and supervisors. Millennials tend to be easily bored and in need of constant stimulation (Rikleen, 2014). Additionally, millennials struggle when their needs are not met or when they feel unfulfilled (Behrens, 2009). The ability of millennials to interact with older generations, especially in face-to-face situations, is lacking (Walmsley, 2011). Millennials tend to fall into an "imposter syndrome" mentality. They may be high-achieving, but there is a feeling of disheartened fear when they think they may not measure up.

Think about it…

How would you describe millennial interactions with older generations in your institution?

_____
_____
_____
_____
_____
_____

How have millennials in your institution changed workplace dynamics?

_____
_____
_____
_____
_____
_____

The "So What" for Higher Education

Despite reluctance to buy into the millennial hype, the characteristics above need consideration from higher education faculty, staff, administration and even boards. While the change in higher ed may not be systemic as a result of the millennial infusion, change, at some level, will be inevitable. The impact of millennials on post-secondary institutions may be marginal at first but, with time, as millennials take over administrative leadership roles, change may be far-reaching. The generation who refuses the status quo, and rebels against "because we've always done it that way", undoubtedly will seek some transition, or evolution, in institutions that typically move at a glacial pace.

Millennials, comparatively, have different expectations for work, for authority, and for relationships. Because of these generational differences, colleges would be remiss to ignore millennial faculty implications on higher education traditions, technology, the role of the faculty member and even infrastructure. The new faculty member, one whose job description and job calling emphasized collaboration and teamwork, very well may become an innovative and creative force.

However, despite positive character traits, the millennial faculty contingent is young and therefore still needs professional and faculty development. It is not enough to assume millennials will gravitate toward traditions of old without a thorough explanation-and even then, they may still push back. Recruiting and retaining millennial faculty must be a university-wide endeavor. The achievement-oriented, connected but distressed Generation Y contingent is coming, like a tidal wave, and universities should be well suited to develop programs that address generational dynamics.

Think about it…

What are some potential implications of millennials on higher education (broadly)?

_____

_____

_____

_____

_____

_____

What are some potential implications of millennials on your institution (specifically)?

_____

_____

_____

_____

_____

_____

The New Professoriate

In some ways, as students, millennials changed higher education. As faculty, they could continue to expand their influence. Yet it should be noted that the institution was already changing before millennials were employed. Unfortunately, a decrease in faculty governance and an increase in faculty role and responsibility could ultimately contribute to a more pronounced shift in educational culture.

In 2009, Evans explained that the duty and expectations of faculty members have become more complex and diverse. Yet, despite increased responsibility, other faculty expectations remain the same, or more demanding. Meaning, new faculty are expected to do more, yet are judged on the same standards and spectrum as past faculty. Austin (2002) believes this next faculty generation must have solid grounding in research and appreciations; understand teaching and learning processes; possess a knowledge of uses of technology in education; appreciate engagement and service; have communication skills appropriate for various audiences; have an expertise in working in diverse groups; appreciate institutional citizenship and related skills; and appreciate the core purposes and values of higher education. These eight essential skills transcend, in some ways, the previous professoriate. The three-pillared stool of teaching, scholarship and service continues to provide faculty with umbrella concepts for succeeding as a faculty member, but new faculty, especially millennial faculty (those who desire increased feedback and specific standards) may want more than the traditional broad strokes categories.

Teaching

Today, faculty members must be adept at using innovative learning methods through unique modalities. Online and hybrid teaching experience has become the norm, not the outlier. Additionally, an ever-increasing understanding of student learning has presented an environment that discourages traditional methods such as lecture. Active-learning, service-learning, experiential learning and self-guided instructor-facilitated exercises have become more prominent. The onus is on professors to recognize that one basic traditional model may not suffice and, instead, multiple strategies and techniques can be used in the classroom.

In some ways, faculty-student interactions have changed as well. In keeping with the millennial understanding of teams and teamwork, instructor-student relationships have become more collaborative. Increased relational instructor-student dynamics, like mentor and advisor, are emphasized more when compared to previous generations. There are numerous calls today for innovative and interdisciplinary curricula as a response to the changing market of higher education but also 21st century workplace needs. The "new" professoriate, then, has increased expectations that go beyond delivering content in a traditional format.

Think about it…

In what ways have teaching expectations changed at your institution within the last (5); (10); (20) years?

_____

_____

_____

_____

_____

_____

Scholarship

Generally, millennials are high-anxiety and high-pressure individuals. As mentioned before, millennials may struggle with symptoms of imposter syndrome. These challenges are apparent in all facets of the new professoriate, but 21st century scholarship expectations continue to place high pressure on millennial faculty members. While scholarship expectations remain high (arguably some institutions have always practiced the publish or perish model), institutional expectations, especially related to the other two faculty categories of teaching and service, can be daunting. Increased teaching expectations can take time, energy and effort that even for the faculty member teaching one course per semester distract from grant applications and published materials. Thankfully, interdisciplinary partnerships have become more popular and institutions are heeding Boyer's (1990) mantra to move beyond the teaching vs. research debate and instead foster environments for a scholarship of teaching and learning. These developments have at least allowed for additional outlets for research.

Think about it…

In what ways have research expectations changed at your institution within the last (5); (10); (20) years?

_____

_____

_____

_____

_____

_____

Service

A 2010 study by Gappa and Austin revealed a startling truth. Today's faculty member works longer hours than their predecessors. Faculty members have long been expected to serve as foundational university citizens. This role includes, among other responsibilities, a governance aspect and the ability to sit on university committees. This need is both financial (as institutions can free up resources by allowing faculty members to serve as decision makers and initiative drivers) but also reflects the very nature of the institution—an environment that, at its core, runs on shared governance. Faculty should participate in mechanisms that highlight their specific interests and reinforce the nature of the institution. Yet, the rise in contingent faculty presents a conundrum for full-time professors. For one, at some institutions, part-time faculty are not expected to participate in service initiatives. This creates a service vacuum as full-time faculty must spread themselves across even more committees. Additionally, as institutions navigate 21st century waters that reinforce alternative revenue sources and the necessity to enhance the student experience, initiatives increase. Thus, fewer faculty members are expected to serve on more committees.

Think about it…

In what ways have service expectations changed at your institution within the last (5); (10); (20) years?

_____

_____

_____

_____

_____

_____

What are a few institutional intricacies that a new faculty member at your university may have trouble understanding or navigating?

_____

_____

_____

_____

_____

_____

Conclusion

Obviously, some generalizations exist in the preceding pages. However, it is ultimately important to remember that, even in the midst of general statements, generations are different, and the professoriate has changed. While the range of the differences and changes is certainly up for debate, it is worth noting that we live in a new-age in higher education. The following chapters in this volume will help further solidify the identity of the new, specifically millennial, faculty member and will provide strategies to develop and engage this unique population for the good of students and to the benefit of the institution.

References

Alton, L. (2018, January 22). Millennials aren't job hopping, young people are: 5 things to keep in mind. Retrieved from https://www.forbes.com/sites/larryalton/2018/01/22/millennials-arent-job-hopping-young-people-are-5-things-to-keep-in-mind/#768e02af10d8

Austin, A. E. (2002). Creating a bridge to the future: Preparing new faculty to face changing expectations in a shifting context. *The Review of Higher Education, 26*(2), 119-144.

Behrens, W. (2009, Spring). Managing millennials: They are coming to a workplace near you. *Marketing Health Services,* 19-21.

Boyer, E. L. (1997). *Scholarship reconsidered: Priorities of the professoriate.* Princeton, N.J.: Carnegie Foundation for the Advancement of Teaching.

Chenkovich, K., & Cates, S. (2016). Welcome to the millennial generation: Should this generation be attracted, managed and retained by corporations differently? *International Journal of Management and Human Resources, 4,* 79-93.

Curran, T., & Hill, A. P. (2019). Perfectionism is increasing over time: A meta-analysis of birth cohort differences from 1989-2016. *Psychological Bulletin, 145,* 410-429. DOI: 10.1037/bul0000138

Evans, D. (2009, September 14). Redefining faculty roles. Retrieved from https://www.chronicle.com/blogs/onhiring/redefining-faculty-roles/8016

Gappa, J. M., & Austin, A. E. (2010). Rethinking academic traditions for twenty-first-century faculty. *AAUP Journal of Academic Freedom, 1,* 1-20.

Morreale, S. P., & Staley, C. M. (2016). Millennials, teaching and learning, and the elephant in the college classroom. *Communication Education*, 65:3, 370-373, DOI: 10.1080/03634523.2016.1177842

Mukherjee, S. (2018, January 4). Millennials are killing yet another thing: Being imperfect. And it's not a good thing. Retrieved from http://fortune.com/2018/01/04/millennials-are-killing-yet-another-thing-being-imperfect-and-its-not-a-good-thing/

Myers, K. K., & Sadaghiani, K. (2010). Millennials in the workplace: A communication perspective on millennials' organizational relationships and performance. *Journal of Business and Psychology, 25*, 225-238. DOI: 10.1007/s10869-010-9172-7

Rikleen, L. S. (2014, February). Where they're coming from. *Communication World, 31*, 14-17.

Strauss, W., & Howe, N. (1991). *Generations: The history of America's future, 1584-2069*. New York: William Morrow and Company.

Schullery, N. M. (2013). Workplace engagement and generational differences in values. *Business Communication Quarterly, 76*, 252-265.

Twenge, J. (2017, September). Have smartphones destroyed a generation? Retrieved from https://www.theatlantic.com/magazine/archive/2017/09/has-the-smartphone-destroyed-a-generation/534198/

Walmsley, A. L. (2011). Closing the communication gap. *Educational Horizons, 90*, 25-26.

Helpful Resources

Strawser, M. G. (Ed.). (2019). *Leading millennial faculty: Navigating the new professoriate*. Lanham, MD: Rowman & Littlefield

Maximizing Millennial Talent in Higher Education Faculty Vignettes

The Only Number That Matters: Reflections of a Young Faculty

Liza Ngenye, Ph.D., La Sierra University, Communication

I was 23 years old when I began teaching as a college faculty member. During my first interview, the Vice Chancellor of a small private university looked at my resume and looked back at me then back at the resume before putting it down on his large mahogany desk. He looked disappointed. "You see…" he began to explain, "Most of our students are mature executives who return to college after a successful career to get the 'paper' and I'm not so sure how they will take you." I promised the Vice Chancellor that I would work harder than the other faculty and wouldn't disappoint him, the students or the institution.

My first class was at 9 am and I got to campus at 5 am. I rehearsed my lecture a million times the night before, in my dreams and while I was driving across town to the university. I wore a black pantsuit, tied my hair into a bun, and put my notes in a briefcase. When I entered the classroom, my students were old enough to be my parents and grandparents. So, I paraded myself and talked about my degrees, clients and work accomplishments, and told them I would only answer to the title 'professor.' I was overcompensating. Worse still, the students could see it, the thing I tried most to hide from them: the only number that mattered was my age.

Best practices for handling the "age question"

If you're a young faculty, age is the only number that matters, not your degrees, accomplishments or lofty achievements. So, how do you navigate the delicate terrain of being young without being obnoxious? Here are three lessons I've learned.

1. Identify the question

When asked, "How old are you?," the typical response of a young faculty is to be combative as if the speaker were trying to undermine an unspoken authority. Asking one's age is not the same as asking if you're good enough, smart enough or accomplished enough. So it's very important to identify what the speaker is asking.

2. Be honest

Therefore, if you're asked about your age, simply answer the question. An honest response communicates to speaker that you're not insecure enough to hide from the facts but instead that you're inviting them to learn more about who you are and how it is you've accomplished so much at such a young age. Honesty is an invitation to have a meaningful interaction.

3. Be humble

There's an African proverb that says, "Wisdom is in the grey hairs." Even though you may have more accomplishments than grey-haired people it doesn't mean you've stopped learning. There is so much more to learn if only you are willing. Remember, when you have your grey hairs you'll have wisdom to share with a young faculty who you will probably question about their age.

Improving Modern Millennial Meetings

Benjamin Drury, Morton College, Sociology

As a millennial faculty member I find myself at odds with a great deal of the existing construct that is higher education. Standardized forms, organizational structure and bureaucracy, orientations, shared governance…some of these aspects of the career that is, in my view, one of equal parts calling and talent, have a deleterious effect on my view of teaching at the University level. Yet if there is one common gripe that is most often cited in conversations of "how's it going" among colleagues of mine at conferences and other professional development opportunities, it is the relentless deluge of meetings that suck the life, power, and interest from the body of your average millennial faculty member. At a time where an ever increasing amount of technology has made face-to-face classroom communication nearly possible and meaningful, it would make sense that we, as educators, would integrate these same strategies in the official goings on of our classrooms, departments, divisions, and universities. Modern meeting strategies at institutions of higher education are in need of some significant care, and it all begins with triage. For those meetings where much of what is achieved could have easily been accomplished through email or other collaborative means, I am suggesting that we consider making use of one (or all) of these three strategies:

1. Talk with your faculty: A great deal of what directly impacts faculty is determined outside of their office, floor, or building. Administrators often set the tone, frequency, and content of meetings. Involving millennial faculty especially in the design and function of modern meetings can give ownership over the form of meetings. By using this strategy, a university can

determine what might be important to the most faculty and use this information to create meetings that are engaging and yield concrete outcomes with consensus.

2. Test out some new technology: Nothing brings millennial faculty to the table faster than a new technology that can be used to improve their working conditions. Well, that and free coffee and baked goods, but that's another story. Regardless of whether or not it would be a product from Apple, a new software engineer, media platform, or device manufacturer, most millennials are interested in learning about new technology and using it in their daily life. Institutions should consider discussing topics of technology with millennial faculty, seeing what they might be interested in learning about, and then investing in it and accompaning training opportunities for all faculty…then actually using it to improve on the duration and covered topics of modern meetings.

3. Hosting online meeting forums: Most higher education institutions have some form of Learning Management System. We can use these platforms to create "courses" for different committees and other agents of institutional change where participants can contribute to discussions, share resources, and create strategies for progressing their specific mission and values. This can also be beneficial in orienting all faculty and participants to a form of technology that is likely costing our institutions thousands of dollars a year…and potentially going underutilized.

Now, I am not saying that all meetings are meaningless. I myself serve on a committee that meets once a week to discuss issues of assessment at our university and find myself looking forward to having meaningful discussions about capturing evidence of student learning and gaps in teaching performance to enhance the overall educational experience for my students. What I am saying is that as new generations start to move into faculty roles at universities, we need to take time to figure out ways to increase opportunities for their productivity…or risk precipitating a negative working environment for many members of the academic community. With a little bit of forethought, inclusion of multiple stakeholders, and attention to the focus and goals of meetings we can improve the form and function of modern meetings to suit the needs of all faculty.

Section II
Who are they?

Millennials treat systems differently, especially compared to their generational predecessors. Even education is not immune to their influence. Millennials, probably to the chagrin of some, will inevitably influence additional aspects of the current higher education system. According to Strawser and Bucalos (2018), higher education "systems" are typically hierarchical, and, in some cases, the hierarchy refuses to change. While this is not necessarily bad, in and of itself, the status quo, when left unchecked, can become ineffective. Millennials, as proponents of the anti-status quo, may feel some higher education policies, procedures and even unwritten rules are archaic and not helpful.

The traditional aspects of higher education may experience a revamping, or at least a re-evaluation, as millennial leaders emerge (Gen X members also challenged the "way things are"—for instance, "X" members have been challenging tenure practices long before millennials). Yet, it is not helpful to rely on "potential" or speculation, as institutions may not see the ramifications of millennial ideas for decades. Instead, the status quo can be approached as something to be re-considered in light of the new higher ed landscape and the changing professoriate. Either way, millennials may not respond positively to some traditional outworking of colleges and universities.

Brown (2016) reminds us that tradition is still present in many institutions, but this tradition may cause millennials consternation. Millennials desire work-life balance and flexibility; in some cases they may refuse to respond to traditional policies and procedures. Additionally, the concept of individual research without interdisciplinary collaboration is foreign to many millennial scholars. Improving these dimensions—flexibility, work-life balance, liberation from traditional policies (for instance, systematic rules for tenure and promotion) and collaborative structures—could cause millennials to view institutions more positively.

As millennials transition from college students to college faculty, a reiteration of their wiring and the connection between generational characteristics to institutional structure is helpful and necessary. While the ramifications of millennial faculty may be undetermined for decades, an initial exploration can help provide a context for faculty developers and university administrators. As Brown (2017) posits in a Chronicle article focused on generations, "their [millennials] influence in academe will continue to grow over the next decade as the youngest ones finish graduate programs and move into the academic workplace, and the older ones take over middle-management roles" (para. 4).

Think about it…

Whether or not you are a millennial faculty member, are there aspects of the system you want to change (not solely for the sake of change, but because you believe they may be inefficient or ineffective)?

_____

_____

_____

_____

_____

_____

Millennials are often defined by common characteristics and collectively they: (a) consider life in circular, hopeful terms; (b) are team players and collaborators; (c) grew up with technology and are tech savvy; (d) are achievement-oriented and socially conscious; (e) were heavily supervised during their upbringing; and (f) are continuous learners and team players who are part of an extremely diverse and highly educated generation (Brack & Kelly, 2012). It is important to come to grips with the nuances of this generation. Thus, the following sections will present information related to how millennials changed higher education as students and their assumed, projected, impact on higher education as faculty and even administrators. First, however, the millennial mindset will be presented as an overarching framework that millennials, albeit generally, possess.

The Millennial Mindset

Faculty developers and administrators would do well to remember that the millennial demographic (those in the 1980/1982-1996 birth year range) are distinct and generationally unique. Yet the millennial mindset is generationally agnostic. There are certain people, no matter their age, that are predisposed to what could be called millennial characteristics. Development, at an institutional level, must address long-standing mindset categories, not just millennial challenges.

Separate from the millennial generation, the millennial mindset is encroaching (and maybe has encroached) upon higher education. The system will continue to change as millennials take power and step in to leadership positions. Prototypical millennial characteristics, such as a desire for work-life balance, flexibility, collaborative opportunities, etc. are not unique to millennials. In fact, other faculty, boomers or members of Generation X, may align more with a millennial mindset than they do their own generational identifiers. How, then, can institutions appropriately engage those most common elements that millennial faculty, or millennial mindset faculty, may desire?

Think about it…

Based on your interaction(s) with millennial faculty members, how does the millennial mindset conflict with current college and university practice?

_____
_____
_____
_____
_____
_____

Millennials as Students

As students, millennials were the first "daily documentation" generation. The advent of the smartphone and social media platforms during millennial formative years allowed this demographic to blend their public and private lives in a uniquely personal way. As such, this generation may be well-equipped to bridge communication gaps with today's modern student (Brown, 2017).

In a 2013 *Time* magazine article, Stein lamented the state of millennials but also called them team players, optimistic, confident, rule-followers, and generally achievement-oriented in everything they do. For millennials, achievement is paramount, and in many cases past achievement has been dictated by team-based projects as well as heavy influence of others (i.e. parents, guardians and teachers).

Often this achievement mentality was spurred on by contexts both natured and nurtured. Millennial parents, those of "helicopter" fame, were heavily involved in the lives of their children and often encouraged self-esteem and self-worth mantras that were not as focused as previous generations. Participation, not just competition, was enforced which led to assumptions that millennials want, and need, recognition for *just showing up*. Parents stressed future preparedness which led to millennial fixations on achievement (Sandeen, 2008).

As millennials entered higher ed campuses in 2000, there was inordinate pressure from millennials themselves and their families. Unlike Gen X, millennial students became part of an institutional environment that redefined academic standards, enjoyed smaller class sizes, employed clear grading processes and fast, constant feedback (Monaco, 2009). Millennial desires for recognition, in life and the classroom, became an illustration for a broader reversion back to a context that was primarily child-centered (Sandeen, 2008).

Unlike their predecessors, millennial college students were more apt to make changes if something was not in line with their expectations. The demanding nature of their parents, and tendency for millennials themselves to have high expectations, led to an increase in student university withdrawals if either party was not satisfied (Monaco, 2009). Universities created streamlined environments for millennial students, with immediate feedback, and learning was fostered by multiple tools and resources. Millennial consumer demands forced colleges and universities to create stronger parent-focused initiatives, specific communication requirements for faculty interactions, and rules for how technology would be used in the classroom.

Cardon (2014) believes millennials wanted to excel in the classroom with minimal effort. This perspective lends itself to a sense of academic entitlement. In some ways, when they were students, universities gave in to millennial demands and established some unrealistic expectations for life outside the academy.

Think about it...

What are other millennial student characteristics that could influence their behavior, or desires, as faculty members?

_____
_____
_____
_____
_____
_____
_____
_____
_____
_____

Generation Z Students

Just like millennials, members of Generation Z will bring about far-reaching institutional questions. Colleges and universities must come to grips with Generation Z characteristics in order to effectively develop and train millennial faculty as they interact with this new student generation. In order to reach Gen Z students, millennial faculty need technical, conceptual and interpersonal skills that can help create a conducive classroom environment.

Members of Generation Z have already been influenced by the Great Recession and the advent of technology including, but not limited to, smartphones and social media platforms. This has created a desire for education that is applied, practical and relevant. Students today expect material that has a high return on investment. As such, millennial faculty will be required to address concerns related to the value of a college degree—questions that traditionalists, boomers and Gen X did not have to explicitly address in classes or advising sessions. Students today are frugal and concerned with value-based purchases.

Generation Z students are constantly connected. They have been impacted by social influencers, not just prototypical celebrities, and they share details of their life via online social networks. However, they are a little more secretive compared to millennials (i.e. Snapchat). This high-tech efficiency pushes them to assume that all others, including faculty, staff and higher education administrators, have a similar tech acumen. Additionally, their desire for, and connection to, technology has impacted their learning style as they prefer learning opportunities that are enhanced by technology and are also visually appealing. This generation prefers face-to-face elements of the traditional classroom mixed with virtual elements that extend into a realm where experiential learning is achieved.

It is also important to note that Generation Z students are

entrepreneurial and opportunistic. They are content creators, not just consumers. They want opportunities to "do" and participate in their learning. In some ways, they want to drive their learning preferences. This entrepreneurial mindset, the willingness to personally engage and not passively consume, will change the higher ed classroom dynamic.

Think about it...

What are other ways Generation Z students will change higher education?

_____

_____

_____

_____

_____

_____

What is most important for millennial faculty to consider as they interact with the modern (Gen Z) student?

_____

_____

_____

_____

_____

_____

Millennials as Faculty

Unfortunately, unlike their predecessors, Millennials tend to be self-focused and less willing to compromise. They are also competitive and assertive with extremely high-performance standards. Positively, Gen Y leaders tend to take risks, are open to new approaches, and have an intensity that tends to energize others. In many ways this shifts the current corporate structure that responded to traditional and boomer leaders who generally minimized risk to ensure predictability, were less emotional and expressive, and were loyal and respectful of authority.

Grappling with millennial faculty differences can serve administrators, staff, and senior faculty alike. While millennial faculty are not unique in every area, they are different in several ways. The following section explores millennial faculty differences from areas of technology, to workplace dynamics and leadership.

Technology

Millennial faculty tend to have a positive response to technology. While technically not digital natives, at least compared to Generation Z, most millennial faculty have, at the very least, been influenced and impacted by technology's overarching presence. For millennials, often referred to as tech-savvy, the integration of efficient tech-systems into their institutions is crucial. Today, millennials embrace technology more noticeably than their generational predecessors and their instinctual response is to use tech-systems to aid their work, meetings and teaching. As such, for new faculty members, institutions are expected to have new and top-of-the-line technology as a recruitment tool but also to help with teaching and research (Smith, 2019).

Connectivity is the overarching purpose for millennial technology. As Wiedmer (2015) states, technology, for millennials, created an environment of social activity and networks that allowed for team-oriented activities. This constant connectivity was satisfying for millennials as they could share opinions and identity at any time. Millennials are now constantly connected within their organizations.

This technological revolution, though, had ramifications for how millennials learned to learn, so to speak, and solve problems (Nimon, 2007). The rapidly changing technology environment, occurring primarily during millennial formative years, altered student interactions with tech platforms. In essence, the faculty member, not the student, was forced to adapt (McHaney, 2011). Technology, for millennial students, exacerbated desires for an active and engaged learning environment, instructor immediacy, and instant/constant feedback. These expectations, which came to fruition in their university classrooms, remain faculty preferences. Millennials are forcing the system to adapt, not the other way around. Technology, with both the efficiency and flexibility it affords, has become a prime illustration for the shift.

As faculty members, the reliance on, and appreciation for technology is unlikely to dissipate for millennials. Status-quo information systems, or inefficient technology use, will probably be rebuffed as this generation explores new ways to stay connected to students, staff and other faculty across their university campus. Universities should consider current technology innovations and incorporate intentional, flexible, and efficient systems that enable collaborative thinking and quick-decision making for faculty members.

Think about it...

What technology "system" is your institution currently using that may be anti-millennial, or, to put it another way, how can your institution use technology more efficiently?

_____

_____

_____

_____

_____

_____

Coaching and Mentorship

Millennials want to be supported and understood. This leads to a desire to be coached and mentored not only by those outside of their professional experience but also by managers, leaders and coworkers. As institutions prepare for the influx of Gen-Y faculty members, a thorough examination of current onboarding procedures, including mentorship and coaching opportunities, should be on the agenda.

Institutions can approach mentorship programs from a variety of perspectives. Cross-generational and cross-disciplinary mentorship can help increase collaboration across campus while also promoting and engaging millennial desires for team-based initiatives. A campus mentoring program can help new faculty understand and acclimate to a university's culture. Intentional mentorship that emphasizes institutional structures and university relationships can help new faculty acculturate and older faculty share decades worth of insights. In a similar vein, two-way mentorship has become more common. Two-way mentorship, otherwise known as reverse mentoring, allows the millennial employee to provide technology training while employees from other generations would provide work and professional advice.

Millennials desire mentorship and feedback from their managers. As a generation that clamors for instant and consistent feedback, Generation Y mentorship can help clarify roles while also providing specific evaluation. Explicit expectations and informal feedback can be pillars of a university mentorship program.

A well-designed mentorship program also encourages millennial faculty to voice concerns they may have in an environment that encourages psychological safety. Millennials want to be heard and have their opinions validated. Providing a space for questions and engagement can help millennials feel connected to the institution and, even more so, provide clarity in a system that can be confusing and stoic. The university administrative system, a traditionally top-down and hierarchical platform, can be difficult to navigate. Thus, mentorship can encourage questions and successful navigation of systemic expectations. Millennials may appreciate the opportunity for feedback and clarity.

Universities can provide purposeful avenues for mentorship and coaching for all faculty, not just millennials. Knowing how one is performing, and understanding specific expectations, are not unreasonable requests. While millennials may cross boundaries and may desire, unrealistically, an inordinate amount of their leader or manager's time to engage in a coaching or mentorship relationship, the embedded desire is positive. However, the structure in which coaching and mentorship occurs can be approached as a means of successful cross-collaboration that emphasizes feedback and formative questions.

Think about it…

Are there mentorship structures (formal or informal) that are already in place at your institution? Discuss their features.

_____

_____

_____

_____

_____

_____

How can your institution develop more concrete, or formal, mentorship opportunities for all faculty?

_____

_____

_____

_____

_____

_____

Collaboration and Interdisciplinary Projects

Millennials are natural collaborators, and, as mentioned above, their success has often been based on team-based endeavors. This creates interesting dynamics in a world like higher education that is traditionally siloed and based on individual merit and accomplishment. Yet this desire for collaboration may be something universities can implement to increase employee job satisfaction and encourage more stellar research, teaching, and service outcomes.

Gardner (2016) does well to remind institutions that this generation wants to collaborate, and it is assumed that collaborative scholarship will be encouraged and facilitated by institutions. As a result of their undergraduate experience that emphasized collaborative team projects and group work, millennial faculty expect collaborative research to not only be an option but to be facilitated by the university in some form.

For millennials, their desire for collaboration has been fueled by exposure to collaborative tech tools. Millennials have grown up with tech hardware and software that create environments for social-networking and connection; as such, this collaborative and team-based mentality has penetrated much of what they do (Crumpacker & Crumpacker, 2007). Facilitated by mindset and technology, millennial faculty crave collaborative initiatives in their institutions.

In essence, the millennial desire for collaborative work is probably based on several driving factors. For one, when the responsibility is shared, one lone individual does not have to bear the brunt of the burden when something goes wrong. Additionally millennials have grown up in a connected world. This connectedness, both the desire for and the ability to relate, has become a driving force for millennials both in how they spend their time and make decisions. Institutions can approach this collaborative mentality reluctantly or with vigor.

Universities should provide resources for faculty members to engage in community-driven collaborative partnerships. It is important for administrators, and institutional structures, to establish and encourage connections between millennial researchers and the community-at-large. Millennials want to solve problems, especially with their research, but they want to do so as part of a team.

Are there ways your institution can develop more collaborative opportunities for faculty in all realms: teaching, service, and research?

_____

_____

_____

_____

_____

_____

Measures, Metrics, and Motivation

The millennial desire for feedback, driven in part by an achievement orientation, has crept into higher education. Millennials do want to know key performance metrics and they desire instant and constant feedback that the system typically does not allow for, or even attempt. Instead, higher education is driven by summative assessment (i.e. annual evaluations, tenure review every third year, and promotions/decisions every six, etc.).

Tenure may very well be one central concern for millennial faculty. Mallard and Singleton (2007) understand that millennials believe teaching and service should be rewarded in promotion and tenure decisions. Academic leaders can encourage a more central understanding of tenure that intertwines teaching, scholarship, service and other measures related to academic work, especially considering the rise of the public academic.

Millennials have become, somewhat by necessity, masters of efficiency. Because of increased expectations in faculty development, student services and student success, as well as teaching expectations more generally, millennials have learned how to maximize and leverage their experiences in one area (i.e. teaching, service or research) by using those experiences to maximize success in other areas. Or, to say it another way, millennials have trained themselves to accomplish multiple objectives with one action (more on this in the next section).

The tenure process, increasingly frustrating for millennials, is certainly not Gen Y friendly. Millennial tenure concerns, including but not limited to vague requirements and outdated standards, lack of guidance and changing, or evolving, administrative policies toward tenure, can create confusion for millennial faculty.

Institutions can collaboratively work with millennial faculty to achieve goals and outcomes that correspond to tenure outcomes. Instead of refusing additional information on requirements, administrators can help clarify process, procedures, and standards. Written guidelines and clear timelines can be helpful for those millennials who want specific metrics. The hope is that clarifying structure and increasing transparency of measuring a "job well done" will cause millennials to avoid frustration about the lack of guidelines and inconsistent feedback.

Think about it...

How does your institution communicate tenure (requirements, process, expectations) to new faculty?

_____
_____
_____
_____
_____
_____

Are there aspects of the tenure process that your institution could clarify or make more "millennial" friendly? If so, what are they?

_____
_____
_____
_____
_____
_____
_____
_____

Rapid Advancement and Workplace Preferences

Millennials value personal growth, personal development, and personal achievement. These desires influence millennial loyalty. Often classified as disloyal, millennials tend to leave organizations early, compared to previous generations, when they notice that an organization is not aligned with their end goal or when an organization does not demonstrate avenues for growth (Pew, 2010).

Millennials have been coined as needy or entitled. The tendency, for some members of Gen Y, is to assume that their workplaces will, and should, mirror their upbringing—a context surrounded by praise, feedback, and a personalized climate that enforces the importance of what they want (Levenson, 2010). Personalized work that leads to rapid advancement is expected.

In 2018, Gallup found that 71% of millennials are disengaged at work. This disengaged mentality can be driven by various factors, but no matter the cause, institutions are not immune to this disengaged mantra. Cullen and Harris (2008) report that institutions with a traditional systemic approach, ambiguous expectations, and unfair practices will tend to be less millennial-friendly and may cause a decline in millennial job satisfaction.

Institutions must create a work environment that connects to millennial values both for change and also for daily tendencies. Millennial desires for flexibility, for instance, will not go away. In fact, generations after millennials may clamor more for flexibility and employee-driven environments.

Millennial engagement may be enhanced by solidifying appropriate expectations and providing a way for advancement in the non-traditional sense. Some millennials expect leadership positions quicker, comparatively. It may be beneficial to allow those who are competent, willing, and able to follow promotional tracks in unorthodox or non-traditional ways.

In what ways can your institution revise workplace expectations to meet evolving millennial desires?

_____

_____

_____

_____

_____

_____

In what ways do you think millennials should relinquish some of their desires that may be unrealistic or unreasonable?

_____

_____

_____

_____

_____

_____

Meaningful Work

Millennials have high-level expectations for work and work outcomes. Tulgan (2009) believes that millennials find entry-level tasks unfulfilling. Their high-esteem and expectations lend themselves to a desire and expectation for challenging and meaningful work.

Millennials have a firm commitment to collaboration and social justice, and their work often connects to civic opportunities. This connection is unique, especially compared to other generations (Gardner, 2016). Generation Y members want to solve research questions and social problems in ways that have tangible impact. For this generation, there is an expectation of greater work-life balance but there is also a different understanding of identity. This means they view issues, personal and professional, in more holistic ways. While there are greater expectations for balance, everything is connected.

Service, for millennial faculty, represents an opportunity that, at least initially, is not burdensome. Instead, service becomes a vehicle for learning about the institution and solving real-world issues. For collaborators, the option to go outside the department and engage is valuable and desired. However, these desires for service go beyond the traditional brick and mortar college as well.

Millennial students were initiated heavily into service and experiential learning opportunities. It would make sense then that as faculty members millennials want to engage their communities through long-term partnerships and initiatives that transcend one specific project. Social change is the desired outcome and millennial faculty believe their research, teaching and service can help solve legitimate social problems.

Think about it…

How can you encourage your institution to consider a more holistic perspective of meaningful work?

_____

_____

_____

_____

_____

_____

Authority and Leadership

As systemic questioners, millennials will continue the trend started by Gen X. While members of Generation X were questioning of authority, they tended to respond positively to "the office" and respect those in positions of power. For millennial faculty, just like when they were students, there is a substantial expectation of those in leadership positions.

Millennial faculty members tend to respect authority figures who approach leadership as a mentorship responsibility. Millennials will respond more positively to those who explain certain actions and engage their followers with a certain level of transparency. Generation Y will also respond positively to leaders with integrity, vision, and intentional transparency (but wouldn't we all?).

Members of Generation Y want to serve under trustworthy leaders. Millennials want to hear their leaders and be heard. This means millennials want a seat at the table, so to speak, and want to know that their ideas will be listened to and acted upon when/ if they are satisfactory. Leaders who continue to function as top-down directors may find millennials reluctant to follow their lead.

There is a balance, however, as some millennials might assume full transparency is always required from leaders and that may not be the case. There are some decisions that lend themselves to discretion (i.e. personnel decisions or decisions that could impact employee morale across the institution). Transparency does not have to be constant, nor does it have to manifest itself from *every* leader in *every* case. For millennials, the knowledge that decisions are made with intentionality and purpose is valuable. Thus, leaders can, and probably should, be as transparent as the situation allows. This means, though, that leader-discretion is paramount. As a whole, millennials respond more favorably to leaders they trust and find competent. Transparency can build credibility and lets faculty members know that a decision was not made in a vacuum and was, instead, considered from various angles.

Think about it…

What advice do you have for a leader who wants to balance discretion and transparency?

_____

_____

_____

_____

_____

_____

Institutional Culture

As a way to recruit and retain millennials, leaders should develop and promote an attractive institutional culture. This institutional culture should focus on salary, benefits, balance, purpose, values, diversity, a solid onboarding, process and employee engagement. A successful institutional culture should also promote flexibility, training and development, growth potential, and open communication. These elements should all be approached while encouraging collaboration, innovation and mutual support. This is all easier said than done.

Many companies now implement 'millennial rules' to recruit, retain and maximize millennial talent. However, in an academic environment, a pool table and dart board seem inappropriate. There are, however, academy-appropriate millennial rules organizations could implement. One specific change, for some institutions, relates to faculty resources. As academics publishing in a high-pressure environment, access to resources, both financial and print/digital, is a non-negotiable for many millennial faculty. Resource allocation is obviously driven in most cases by institutional ability, but universities can consider where resources for faculty research can be developed and enhanced.

For millennial faculty, higher education may be frustrating because of the traditional elements that define the culture and the fact that institutions are typically reluctant to change. Millennials expect, somewhat rightly, that they will change systematic cultural norms and organizational culture at large (Swenson, 2008)-and they may as they become leaders. Yet cultural definition and implementation, for most institutions, has been a decades long process.

Ultimately, though, implementing millennial rules may not save the institution from millennial career shifts or job-hopping. It is well-documented that this generation will tend to showcase a lack of company loyalty. However, encouraging volunteerism and public scholarship as part of the tenure and promotion process, flexibility, and clear organizational core values can resonate with Generation Y. Throughout the job search process, prospective faculty members, and participants on the search committee, should discuss institutional fit as it relates to institutional culture.

Think about it...

How would you define the culture of your institution?

_____

_____

_____

_____

_____

_____

In what way(s) is your institution's culture counter to mainstream millennial thinking?

_____

_____

_____

_____

_____

_____

Faculty Challenges

Millennial faculty may experience several challenges including institutional fit and frustration with the status quo. But there are other dimensions that need to be addressed that may contribute to millennial concern. Millennial faculty, those of the high-anxiety ilk, may experience issues related to impostor syndrome and mental health concerns. In addition, as advocates and ambassadors of the institution, millennial faculty may find the current higher education landscape challenging as they deal with a cultural negativity toward higher education. The two concerns below are not exhaustive; rather they provide additional items to consider when engaging millennial faculty.

Impostor Syndrome

Millennial faculty preferences and challenges, as presented above, pale somewhat in comparison to a large-scale millennial issue. Millennials, plagued by self-assessment, struggle substantially with imposter syndrome. Impostor syndrome, originally coined by Clance and Imes (1978), is defined generally by McAllum (2016) as a deep-seated insecurity that the individual cannot complete certain tasks or achieve certain goals. To put it another way, those with impostor syndrome consider themselves a fraud.

Generally, around 70% of individuals report feeling like an impostor at least once (Gravois, 2007). However, impostor syndrome may be more pressing and discouraging for those in higher education—a traditionally high-achieving and competitive context. Millennials place themselves under constant pressure. Their high-achieving and accomplishment first mentality creates, in some cases, devastating repercussions. The traditionally individualistic, outcome-driven institution that is higher ed is typically against the team-based, shared responsibility mantra of millennials. They are forced, in their institutions, to create narratives that showcase their individual accomplishments and deliverables. Institutions should consider this reality, especially as impostor syndrome can lead to other mental health issues for faculty members.

Think about it...

What are some ways your institution can help millennial faculty deal with imposter syndrome?

_____

_____

_____

_____

_____

_____

Sustainability

Generation Y faculty may have to deal with long-term sustainability concerns related to higher education. Generation Z students are more likely than previous generations to question the value of a college degree. Their financial security is one of their foremost concerns. Generation Z students also have an extremely practical view of college. The point is not to visit college for enlightenment; rather the point is to graduate and get a job.

What does this do to an institution that has been reluctant to change and finds itself in an identity crisis? Much, unfortunately. Millennial faculty may be concerned with the long-term status of higher education. It (the institution as a whole) is definitely not the stalwart it was when X and boomers entered as employees. Instead, there is far-reaching distrust of universities and colleges. Millennials have to position not just themselves as experts, but their institutions as credible and worth the investment. The current climate, that of a negative landscape surrounding higher education rife with financial concerns and declining student enrollment (amongst increasing competition) can cause millennial faculty even higher anxiety.

Think about it...

How is your institution equipping all faculty (not just millennials) to deal with questions related to the value of obtaining a college degree?

_____

_____

_____

_____

_____

_____

Conclusion

As millennial faculty become millennial administrators, it will be interesting to see how higher education evolves—or where it might take a step backward. No matter how institutions approach millennial faculty, the reality is millennial influence will only increase. Institutions can maximize millennial talent and encourage millennial faculty to thrive. A thoughtful consideration of millennial expectations and characteristics can help colleges and universities recruit, retain, and maximize millennial faculty talent.

References

Bertalanffy, L. (1968). *General system theory: Foundations, development, applications.* New York: George Braziller.

Brack, J., & Kelly, K. (2012). Maximizing millennials in the workplace. UNC Kenan-Flagler Business School. Retrieved from https://www.kenan-flagler.unc.edu/executive-development/custom-programs/~/media/DF1C11C056874D-DA8097271A1ED48662.ashx

Brown, S. (2016, July 22). When millennials become managers. *Chronicle of Higher Education.* p. B4.

Cardon, L. S. (2014). Diagnosing and treating millennial student disillusionment *Change, 46,* 34-40.

Clance, P. R., & Imes, S. A. (1978). The imposter phenomenon in high achieving women: Dynamics and therapeutic interventions. *Psychotherapy: Theory, Research and Practice, 15,* 241-247.

Crumpacker, M., & Crumpacker, J. D. (2007). Succession planning and generational stereotypes: Should HR consider age-based values and attitudes a relevant factor or a passing fad? *Public Personnel Management, 36,* 349-369.

Cullen, R., & Harris, M. (2008). Supporting new scholars: A learner-centered approach to new faculty orientation. *Florida Journal of Educational Administration and Policy, 2,* 17-28.

Gallup. (2018). *How millennials want to work and live.* Retrieved from https://www.gallup.com/workplace/238073/millennials-work-live.aspx

Gardner, S. K. (2016). Mentoring the millennial faculty member, *Department Chair, 27*(1), 6-8.

Levenson, A. R. (2010). Millennials and the world of work: An economist's perspective. *Journal of Business and Psychology, 25,* 257-264.

Mallard, K. S., & Singleton, A. (2007). Creating a responsive community and leading millennial faculty. *Department Chair, 18*(1), 6-8.

McAllum, K. (2016). Managing imposter syndrome among the "Trophy Kids": Creating teaching practices that develop independence in millennial students. *Communication Education, 65,* 363-365.

McHaney, R. (2011). *The new digital shoreline: How web 2.0 and millennials are revolutionizing higher education.* Sterling, VA: Stylus.

Monaco, M. (2009). The flight of the millennials in higher education. *Athletic Therapy Today, 14,* 21-26.

Nimon, S. (2007). Generation Y and higher education: The other Y2K. *Journal of Institutional Research, 13,* 24-41.

Pew Research Center. (2010). *Millennials: A portrait of generation next.* Retrieved from http://assets.pewresearch.org/wp-content/uploads/sites/3/2010/10/millennials-confident-connected-open-to-change.pdf

Sandeen, C. (2008). Boomers, xers and millennials: Who are they and what do they really want from continuing education. *Continuing Higher Education Review, 72,* 11-31.

Strawser, M. G., & Bucalos, A. (2018). Mentoring millennial faculty for success. In A. Atay & M. Z. Ashlock (Eds.), *Millennial culture and communication pedagogies: Narratives from the classroom and higher education.* Lanham, MD: Rowman & Littlefield.

Stein, J. (2013, May 20). Millennials: The me me me generation. Retrieved from https://time.com/247/millennials-the-me-me-me-generation/

Swenson, C. (2008). Next generation workforce. *Nursing Economics, 26,* 60-65.

Tulgan, B. (2009). *Not everyone gets a trophy: How to manage Generation Y.* San Francisco, CA: Jossey-Bass.

Wiedmer, T. (2015). Generations do differ: Best practices in leading traditionalists, boomers, and generations X, Y and Z. *Delta Kappa Gamma Bulletin, 82(1),* 51-58.

Who are they? Faculty Vignettes

The Immigrant Millennial Faculty: The Niche within a Niche

Aditi Paul, Pace University, Communication

There are certain issues that are unique to millennial faculty members who are first generation immigrants. Two that top the list are navigating legal immigration status in the US (alongside tenure) and the struggles of being relatable to American Gen-Z students.

Navigating Legal Status

The fear of being displaced from the US really heightens during the final year of our doctoral program as we *must* get a job within a certain number of days after graduation, or else we lose our legal status and are forced to leave the country. This fear does not automatically go away after getting a job. The work visa that the US government grants us is valid for only 3 years, following which our employers have to re-submit the application authorizing us to work for another 3 years. This process continues until we have earned our permanent residency and eventually citizenship.

Thus it is essential to have institutional support to navigate this tedious immigration process, especially when faculty members are working toward qualifying for tenure. It is also necessary to have people in the administration who can provide emotional support for the immigrant millennial faculty and ensure their well-being. I was lucky enough to have found both at Pace University. Yet in

2018, I found myself in a precarious situation. By the end of the third year of my employment, Pace University had applied for the extension of my work visa, but because of a backlog in the United States Customs and Immigration System, the approval of papers got significantly delayed. This put me at a risk of losing my job. I discussed this issue with my Department Chair who then reached out to the Dean's office. Within a week's time, the Associate Dean informed me that they had decided to pay a certain fee to expedite the process of getting the papers approved. Two weeks from that day, I had my work visa in hand. The way the administration took care of this situation in a timely manner and the way they prioritized my mental peace and well-being made me feel appreciated and valued as an employee.

The Art of Being #relatable

Gen Z students value relatability. They like it when professors make the course content #relatable and are also #relatable as a person. When you hail from another culture and generation, it becomes rather challenging to master this art of relatability. Thus, as immigrant millennial faculty, we end up expending our resources working on things that might be of little concern to our American counterparts. For instance, a Chinese colleague from a Midwestern university confided, "I often spend more time practicing *how to teach*, aka "talk" about course content, anecdotes, etc." This tiny interaction with her showed me the importance of providing a safe space to immigrant millennial faculty members where we can talk about, discuss, and find solutions to these issues in order to succeed as a niche academic community. Maybe it is time to petition for an *immigrant millennial faculty affairs committee*.

Section III
Teaching and Learning

The traditional "game" has changed. Faculty expectations are more rigid. As student desires and needs have evolved, the acumen and skillset of the modern-day faculty member are more involved. Student expectations have changed dramatically since millennial students entered college. Students expect course material to be relevant and timely, and this expectation will be more prevalent as Generation Z students invade college classrooms.

Students today are busy. They want flexible course design and appreciate non-traditional modalities (i.e. online, hybrid/blended course options). This desire for student flexibility places great pressure on faculty members to transcend brick-and-mortar lecture-style. Instead there is a consumeristic expectation of students, and probably rightfully so, that expects instructional strategy tailored to individual learning preferences.

Instructors, then, face significant pressure. Professors remain front line defenders of the academy. Yet in light of these expectations, some institutions remain committed to practices that may be out of date or ineffective. As Evans (2016) warns us, we (higher education) may have entered a spiral that will likely reduce the quality of undergraduate education.

As instructors prepare for academic careers, they must accumulate knowledge in some capacity about the teaching and learning process. For instance, professors must understand learning styles, or preferences, especially of diverse student populations. Unlike ever before, there is an increased expectation of teaching technique rather than just subject-matter expertise. However, professors are still expected to understand and note the intricacies of their discipline and communicate those nuances to novice learners. Furthermore, we are an information-society. Information transfer happens at the click of a button, or the swipe of a screen. What, then, is the role of the former oracle, the professor? These times are not troubling, but they do beg several questions.

Institutions should explore options to enhance teaching and learning skills of their faculty members. This section will broadly address innovation in teaching and learning, as well as discuss innovation and informed teaching practices. Additionally, Scholarship of Teaching and Learning will be positioned as a framework for developing and motivating faculty, especially millennial faculty members.

Think about it…

How have teaching-specific expectations changed in the last two decades?

_____

_____

_____

_____

_____

_____

Teaching and Learning

Teaching and learning initiatives have changed dramatically as new student populations continue to encourage and demand innovative teaching methods. The very nature of student expectations has changed. Not only do students want accessible and relevant content, but students assume higher education will serve as a training ground for ensuing professions. While this has always been the case, the vocational emphasis has become transcendent.

This vocational dynamic has created a veiled training and development approach in higher ed. In some ways, corporations can assume job training, especially for professional degree programs. The emphasis on technical skills has created additional expectations for faculty members. In this technical age, content must be relevant as students are concerned about return on investment and getting hired immediately upon graduation.

Because of these new student requirements, a true teaching and learning approach at all institutions, not just "traditional" teaching universities, is crucial. This section will explore teaching and learning through the lens of the 21st century student and the changing nature of teaching and learning initiatives.

The 21st Century Student

Who is the 21st century student? This question has become more difficult to answer as generational differences become less easily defined and technology continues to penetrate all facets of our lives. As so many have written before, gone are the days of the Sage on the Stage. Student attention spans, and the tools available for information transfer have, in essence, shifted the role of the instructor to that of learning guide or facilitator.

The modern student, at least at the time of this writing, believes that information can be launched, search, distributed, and created within seconds. The vast wealth of knowledge available online transcends that of any specific individual. The goal of teaching, then, is less about transference, that is making sure that you receive a certain concept through the professor. It has to be. Students are generally aware of how to search for answers and less aware how to apply answers or think critically about the answers they are given. As such, instructors become vehicles not for concepts, but for application, relevancy, reasoning, and logic. The problem is that we teach how we were taught. Millennial faculty, the cusp of the facilitation-instruction generation, may still resonate with a lecture-style teaching mentality.

Not only do students expect different outcomes, but they assume they will have unique modes to carry their outcomes forward. Student desires (and not just from traditional students by the way) for flexibility and a consumer-created learning experience have removed the onus from traditional physical spaces and brick-and-mortar campuses. The assumption for instructors, then, is that they will not only understand how to facilitate and guide, but that they will know how to facilitate in various modalities: online, face-to-face, and blended environments.

Current students, digital natives in their own right, assume that technology will not only be present in their courses but that it will have an active and enhanced role. Students want technology and active tools in their courses and will gravitate to classes and instructors who will provide tech-enhanced instruction.

Think about it...

How would you define the 21st century student?

_____

_____

_____

_____

_____

_____

The Changing Landscape of Teaching and Learning

Teaching and Learning Centers have become campus "hubs" for innovation. Centers, at one time, focused on a technology infusion, creating a safe space for faculty to navigate and integrate new technology. Yet, teaching has become more holistic, the center has become an illustration of that new dynamic.

Technology has, of course, remained a teaching and learning topic of conversation, but what was once an *integrate at all costs* mantra has become a *use effectively and efficiently* campaign. This shift has occurred, in part, because of digital-friendly faculty and because of student tech considerations. It is no longer enough to infuse technology; its use and purpose must be clear and intentional.

Course development initiatives, faculty reading and learning groups, and programs that lead (or enable) campus strategic initiatives and innovation have become part of the faculty development identity. As faculty members become more responsible for ensuring student success, beyond traditional "grades", the university must explore development programming that is audience centered and strategic.

Faculty are under constant pressure to improve their courses. As instructors face challenges related to new student demographics and learning styles, some universities have recognized that a renewed emphasis on teaching can contribute to student success.

Faculty roles have expanded because student expectations

of faculty members have increased. Teaching is still considered one leg of the three-legged stool but, as university competition continues to become more intense, student return-on-investment, and ultimately classroom experience, have propelled teaching and learning into a new strata.

Evans (2016) reports that faculty duties have become more diversified and more complex. Faculty, many with limited training, are primarily responsible for assessment. In addition, expectations for undergraduate research have increased. Obligations, like human resource related trainings, have become more common. Ultimately, faculty load and duties have substantially increased (Evans, 2016).

New faculty enter campus with certain skills. Some are more prepared than others to teach effectively. This reality is not new. Preparation in graduate school, and within disciplines, has always differed; it is hard, and has always been hard, to know what to expect of new faculty. Faculty development initiatives, in order to address innovative faculty, must prepare accordingly. However, sadly most leaders have made generational issues a low priority (Cahill & Sedrak, 2012).

Think about it…

In what ways have you seen your institution emphasize teaching in the last decade?

_____

_____

_____

_____

_____

_____

Combining all Worlds: Scholarship of Teaching and Learning

Based on increased teaching expectations and millennial faculty desire for feedback, institutions may consider more intentionality with efforts related to the scholarship of teaching and learning. For context, Bishop-Clark and Dietz-Uhler (2012) defined the scholarship of teaching and learning as "the study of teaching and learning and the communication of findings so that a body of knowledge can be established" (p. 1). But the scholarship of teaching and learning, or SoTL as it is affectionately known, goes beyond scholarly teaching and involves systematic study of teaching and/or learning. This systematic study can provide answers for deep-rooted questions about teaching and/or learning. For millennial faculty, SoTL is one way to combine teaching, research, and service expectations while informing data-driven teaching decisions.

Millennials, natural question-askers, may enjoy the opportunity to think through challenges and successes related to their teaching. SoTL allows millennial faculty to consider why a teaching strategy worked (or fell flat), what changes are necessary to adjust the strategy for the future, and then, ultimately, to share their information to contribute to the broader body of knowledge.

Weimer (2006) believes SoTL has several benefits, many of which are directly applicable to millennial faculty. For Weimer (2006), the exploration of interesting questions, opportunity for deeper learning and consideration, interdisciplinary nature of the movement, and the ability to try and build something new are all benefits of benefits of the scholarship of teaching and learning that may resonate with millennial scholar-teachers. Members of Generation Y also tend toward an imposter syndrome mentality (Pedler, 2011), so SoTL may help establish a solid reason for teaching practice for those who may question instructional decisions or abilities (Savory, Burnett, & Goodburn, 2007).

In *Scholarship Reconsidered,* an oft-cited resource that reinforces the scholarly rigor of the scholarship of teaching and learning, Boyer (1990) proposes that America's colleges and universities need a fresher, more capacious vision of scholarship. Boyer (1990) says that [we] should "set out a new paradigm that views scholarship as having four separate but overlapping dimensions: the scholarship of discovery, the scholarship of integration, the scholarship of application, and the scholarship of teaching" (p. 9). As faculty members face increased expectations of their time in all facets, not just teaching, it is important to consider, or reconsider, how millennial faculty can function effectively in the academy. As such, providing SoTL resources in the academy, especially in graduate school, can help millennial faculty consider how their engagement in the classroom can also inform scholarly practice.

Preparation in Graduate School

In 2002, Austin argued that graduate preparation for the professoriate is lacking. She notes:

> Various pressures and expectations external to and within higher education are creating a time of significant change. The changes within the academy have a direct impact on the work and lives of faculty members. New expectations require the next generation of faculty members to have a range of abilities, skills, knowledge and understanding that go beyond what entering faculty members typically have had. The preparation of the next generation of faculty members cannot be *business as usual*. (p. 128)

While institutions do grasp some of these new expectations, we have seen even more change in the academy since the early 2000s. This begs the question, what can we do to prepare millennial faculty members for the academy while they are in graduate school?

Graduate programs must lead and mentor their students in such a way that they can become valuable members of the new professoriate. Because of the unique wiring of millennial faculty, our institutions need to teach students in graduate school how to: (a) navigate "systems" in higher ed (systems that are at once traditional and hierarchical); (b) respect and respond to authority, even when the authoritative figure may not be transparent, competent or credible; (c) be prepared for unclear and minimal expectations; and (d) be prepared for different communication trends and expectations.

Thankfully, advising in graduate school has become more akin to mentorship. This mentorship process should take into consideration one's desire or aptitude for higher education. Some millennial graduate students are opting to pursue other opportunities beyond the traditional tenure-track faculty position (Brown, 2017). There are fewer tenure-track jobs available and greater competition, which means graduate students may likely end up at teaching institutions, if they pursue the academy at all, rather than R1 institutions. Graduate schools must continue to foster a level of teaching engagement for their students. As Monzo and Mitchell (2018) claim:

> Very few programs take time to teach their graduate students how to teach. Grad students may serve as teaching assistants — though research assistantships are more prestigious, of course — but the main skill they learn in that position is how to grade lots of papers in a short amount of time. (Hint: it usually doesn't involve in-depth feedback.) Then, once someone has passed the comprehensive exams, she might be eligible to teach a class on her own, but it's often seen as wasted energy. (para. 7)

However, the new crop of students, those of the Gen Z ilk, require innovative and data-driven teaching strategies. Members of Gen Z want transparent teaching with explicit real-world connections. Instructors, unless they are trained to function and teach in this way, may not naturally know how to teach material that is practical and applicable using innovative strategy that is driven by research. Members of Generation Z are entrepreneurial, and they want their professors to facilitate the conversation and help establish hands-on activities that provide a logical connection to their future professions. Practically, as institutions prepare future faculty in graduate school, they can include a required class on how to teach undergrads while presenting opportunities for graduate students to teach on their own, not just grade (Monzo & Mitchell, 2018).

Solidifying a firm teaching preparation program in graduate school will help future faculty develop an innovative teaching mentality and will provide an opportunity for exploration and instructional development.

Innovation

In 2016, Sweet, Blythe, and Carpenter posited that we are in the age of innovation. Higher education is changing rapidly, and institutions must adapt quickly. Firmly planted in this age of innovation, institutions must approach teaching and faculty development with a renewed sense of purpose and a new set of eyes.

Innovation is an important conversation topic for all institutions. This is due in part to millennial faculty rebellion against the status quo, but also because the landscape requires, if not demands, innovative decisions. The millennial mindset runs counter to older cultural distinctions about communication, tech use and implementation, as well as business hours and instead focuses on efficiency, productivity, and engagement (Brown, 2016). The classroom, then, has the tendency to become a think tank as well as a task factory.

As "questioners", those who tend to doubt the organization before devoting their loyalty to the organization's goals and mission, millennials will ask why and the "because that's how we have always done it" answer will not suffice. Innovative institutions can respond to millennial cultural expectations while also preparing their systems for modern student expectations. Millennials, whether institutions want it (or like it), will bring change. Unfortunately, in many ways colleges and universities are not designed, systemically or practically, to be flexible.

Innovation requires reorientation. Millennials tend toward collaboration; while previous generations would primarily focus on their own departments, millennials generally recognize that conversing and interacting across academic departments and units can help establish new non-traditional solutions.

Opportunities should be granted to allow millennial faculty to develop a range of teaching skills while also broadly discussing the professoriate. While institutions may be resistant to change, there is hope that some stoic or ineffective practices may be overcome with innovative and creative problem-solving.

While the word "innovation" is often used on college campuses, even during a challenging higher education landscape there should be freedom to uncover new ideas. As such, innovation, especially in the realm of teaching and learning, should be a focus for faculty developers and administrators. Enacting new ideas, even if they are not revolutionary, as well as a new lens and methodology to complex teaching problems and programs should be a central focus for leaders moving forward.

Millennials can be a valuable resource for new ideas and innovative problem-solving. While the focus here is on teaching and learning, it may behoove administrators to consider how millennials can influence innovative thinking across campus. At the very least institutions can encourage millennial faculty to engage in innovative pedagogy and transcend the status quo in their classrooms.

Innovative Pedagogy

As millennial faculty prepare for the new professoriate, it is important for administrators to consider how they are advising this generation and how they are offering feedback. Millennial faculty want feedback on their service, scholarship and teaching. The opportunity to provide explicit feedback and help new faculty think about innovative pedagogy is exciting. Millennials want to know how their teaching will be evaluated. But the good news is that because of certain millennial wiring, Gen Y faculty may willingly use innovative instructional strategy and modalities. Millennials are interested in unique pedagogy like learning communities, community engagement and service learning (Rikleen, 2012). The following list of modern teaching practices are millennial-friendly and relevant for modern students and instructors.

Millennial-Friendly Modalities

Online and Hybrid Modalities

Younger millennials and members of Generation Z are online consistently throughout the day. This online existence has reinforced a desire, and a need, for online and hybrid (blended modalities that emphasize face-to-face and online course components) modalities. With that said, millennial faculty may appreciate the flexible environment online and blended courses offer. Generation Z students prefer classes have either an online component or an added emphasis on technology. Thankfully millennial professors, those who had similar, although less pronounced concerns as their students, recognize that absorption does not occur through lecture.

Enrollment in flexible modalities continues to grow. For instance, from fall 2015 to fall 2016 the number of students participating in an online course grew 5.6% and, at last count, over 6.5 million students in the United States have taken an online course (Friedman, 2018). For obvious reasons, busy-schedules, the desire for flexibility, an increase in tech efficacy, etc., students desire flexible course modalities that, at the very least, incorporate online elements.

Millennial faculty, because of their predisposition to technological advancements (both software and hardware), are well-suited to design and teach online and hybrid courses. Some institutions are still resistant to online and hybrid classes, but when online and hybrid courses are offered you should encourage millennial faculty to, at the very least, teach a course using one of those modalities.

Online and hybrid courses allow millennials to use their tech-savvy wiring to build rapport with students and design a course that adequately addresses learning objectives beyond a traditional brick-and-mortar classroom. Faculty developers and administrators who do encourage development and instruction of online courses should consider how faculty are evaluated. Student feedback, because it is not instantaneous, may be confusing or conspicuously absent. Institutions should continue to require millennial faculty training in flexible modalities, even if as students these same faculty participated in online classes. Encouraging flexible modalities and present opportunities for millennials to teach in online and hybrid environments will benefit institutions.

Think about it...

Based on millennial characteristics, are there some elements of online or hybrid courses that millennial faculty may not find appealing?

_____

_____

_____

_____

_____

_____

_____

_____

Millennial-Friendly Teaching Framework

Experiential Learning

In 1984, Kolb developed what has become a foundational educational framework. Experiential learning theory, in Kolb's mind, reasons that knowledge is created through experience. The process for Kolb, one of experience, thinking, reflecting and acting, takes students on a journey that explores knowledge construction through real-life experience.

Young millennials and Generation Z want to actively participate in their learning. As such, experiential learning, or learning through experience, has become an innovative pedagogical framework for faculty. Institutions can help support faculty members by providing a means to achieve experiential learning both inside and outside the classroom walls. Experiential learning, a broad umbrella that includes service learning, internships, and other modes, emphasizes learning-by-doing. Concrete experience, for the learner, is primary.

When millennials were traditional college students, they wanted experiential classroom methods that were active, not passive. The shift away from passive pedagogy was the model for some millennial faculty members. Because of this experience, millennial faculty are well-suited to explore experiential methods more fully in their own classrooms as instructors.

Students today, those of the Gen Z ilk, still want experiential methods. Universities should encourage their faculty to implement active and experiential methods but, as with all innovative strategies, institutions should not assume that experiential learning objectives will be fostered naturally to millennial faculty. Instead, encourage millennial faculty to explore activities in class that move beyond traditional lecture style underpinnings. Faculty development programming can include "how-to" sessions on fieldwork, simulations, lab-based projects, client-based projects, case studies, and other strategies.

Think about it…

How can your institution prepare millennial faculty to employ experiential learning methodologies in the classroom?

_____

_____

_____

_____

_____

_____

_____

_____

Millennial-Friendly Pedagogy

High-Impact Practices

High-impact practices, initially coined by Kuh (2008), include programs like the first-year experience, learning communities, service learning, internships, and capstone experiences. High-impact practices, otherwise known as HIPs, are designed to engage students in deeper-level thinking, increase student engagement, and improve retention.

HIPs tend to benefit students from a variety of backgrounds and may help create equitable learning environments for students who may be underrepresented. But HIPs, when designed effectively, can positively impact all students in some capacity. The Association of American Colleges and Universities (2018) lists the following as high-impact practices:

- First-Year Experiences
- Common Intellectual Experiences
- Learning Communities
- Writing-Intensive Courses
- Collaborative Assignments and Projects
- Undergraduate Research
- Diversity/Global Learning
- ePortfolios
- Service Learning, Community-Based Learning
- Internships
- Capstone Courses and Projects

Each HIP is unique and can contribute to a positive student

climate. However, millennial faculty, those who are digital-friendly, yearn for meaningful work, and appreciate collaborative and experiential learning, may be encouraged to engage more deeply in specific initiatives that resonate with their personal and professional desires, like high-impact practices.

Learning Communities

Learning communities, by design and implementation, are collaborative. The main purpose of a learning community is a unified educational experience that tackles big picture questions and provides participants with shared required courses and, in many cases, a living experience that is more communal. The expectation is that students are more involved with their professors, solving problems collaboratively. Common themes and common topics are typically explored during learning community initiatives.

On college campuses, learning communities can help foster deep learning and student engagement. Learning communities are valuable because they can create an active and collaborative learning environment that creates deep and long-lasting relationships with faculty through value-added educational experiences.

Through learning communities, millennial faculty can engage in mentorship relationships with students. The learning community environment can establish the instructor-as-facilitator, a role millennial faculty prefer in higher education contexts. The collaborative and communal nature of learning communities can establish a deeper connection with millennial faculty and their students, as well as build rapport between the two parties.

Diversity/Global Learning

As a high-impact practice, universities that establish diverse or global learning experiences create an environment where their students can interact with different cultures and worldviews. In diverse/global learning courses, co-curricular activities or initiatives, students explore difficult and challenging social issues and differences like race, gender, inequality, power, etc. These experiences can occur in the U.S. or students can also engage in international opportunities.

Gen Y faculty are socially active. They are concerned about social injustice. Learning experiences that provide opportunities for students to consider issues of injustice or inequality can encourage deep learning. As institutions consider diverse learning initiatives, it may be wise to ask millennial faculty to lead these initiatives or, at the very least, participate. Diverse or global learning can help millennial faculty reach students while also considering their own social stances on issues of power and inequality.

ePortfolios and Digital Media

Students believe technology (when used appropriately in the classroom) helps them succeed. The days of banning classroom technology, or personal devices, has probably come and gone. However, technology can be used to propel student work into a higher stratosphere. For one, ePortfolios can be implemented for various higher ed purposes. As a high-impact practice, ePortfolios enable students to electronically collect their work over a certain amount of time. Students can then reflect on their own improvement or growth and then share their portfolio with potential employers or their professors. ePortfolios can help students and instructors work together, through electronic means, to present an overview of learning outcome achievement.

ePortfolios, though, are just one way millennial faculty can implement technology in their courses. In addition, millennial instructors can holistically develop digital media activities and assignments.

Gamification, or the use of game-elements in non-game contexts, has become more popular in college classrooms (and K-12 contexts as well). Gamification can motivate and encourage millennial faculty to think differently about how they transfer information and encourage student learning.

Millennial faculty may also appreciate the integration of holistic devices in their classrooms. The Internet of Things, or increased interconnectivity and data generation by devices, as well as the broader wearable technology movement, can satisfy millennial faculty thirsts for data-driven decisions and tech-based education. In a similar vein, tech-savvy millennials may also appreciate opportunities to integrate artificial intelligence or virtual reality into their classrooms, assuming the university can provide the appropriate resources.

Service Learning

Service learning resounds with experiential or field-based opportunities. Typically, community partners and collaborative initiatives are developed. Students generally take course concepts and apply those issues to current problems in their community or world. The end goal, of course, is the application of course material to real-world problems. Students then, with their instructor, reflect on the problem(s) and the solution(s). Service and community learning tends to resonate with millennial faculty because of the emphasis on giving back and the development of value-based work.

Service learning is not unique nor is it "new", but as millennial faculty and students attempt to co-create educational environments, service learning and community-based initiatives may become a vehicle for instruction and facilitation. Millennials and Generation Z are invigorated by developments that solve real-world issues. The ability to take classes beyond four traditional walls is appealing for millennial faculty because they can engage with the community and collaboratively investigate solutions with their students. Universities can encourage service learning by continuing to develop community partnerships and by providing resources for faculty to create programs and initiatives that transcend the classroom context. Service learning will help millennial faculty see additional value, meaning and even fit in their work. A secondary benefit includes faculty members positioning themselves as public scholars and advocates, when appropriate.

Millennial-Friendly Curricula

21st Century Skills/Workplace Demands

Unfortunately, one of the new corporate mantras is the lack of preparation from college graduates (Harrison, 2017). Work, and the resulting expectations of an increasingly "technical" and skill-based marketplace, has changed. Employer expectations of college graduates have changed as well. Employer expectations include, but are not limited to, value-added analytical skills, outcome-based education that in essence trains employees to adapt to corporate cultures, communication skills, technology-efficiency, advanced critical reasoning (Harrison, 2017). Employers assume, in some cases, that college graduates will be prepared to immediately step into a specific corporate context. This expectation results in differed onboarding and employee training.

Students are asking questions related to return on college investment and major/discipline translation at a rapid pace. The exponential increase of college tuition and exorbitant student debt should make students pause and reflect on their educational needs and desires. In an effort to address some of these concerns, the role and function of the career center on most campuses has shifted and institutions are fiercely looking for answers.

The shift should not end with the career center. There must be a continual assessment of college curricula and, while institutions should not succumb to all of the demands of the modern workplace, colleges and universities should at the very least assess the relevance of courses and programs. How does this new phenomena impact millennial faculty?

First, millennial faculty must be adept to address concerns about college cost and the investment, as well as being adept at answering questions related to degree/major connection and workplace expectations. The demand for this type of response has become resounding. Second, millennial faculty can rethink their courses and pedagogy in light of this skill-based expectation. Administrators can help faculty members examine curriculum to determine if their objectives meet the needs of the modern workplace.

Motivation and Teaching

All instructors should assess their course offerings to ensure student outcomes are engaging, applicable, and relevant. Additionally, all instructors should consider how their courses improve student learning. These mandates are not unique to millennial faculty. Yet as colleges continue to identify innovative teaching and learning, millennial faculty can be catalysts for continued exploration.

With that said, administrators should recognize and encourage the millennial response to the status quo, at the very least in the classroom. One of the most maligned millennial traits may in fact be one of the most beneficial in the classroom. As millennials refuse to accept "the way things are" (for a number of reasons), administrators and faculty developers can engage this rebellious thinking and encourage adaptation and evolution in the classroom. It is difficult to determine how student and workplace expectations will continue to change in the future, but institutions can use the anti-status-quo mentality of millennial faculty to push against traditional pedagogy as well as normative teaching and learning.

Millennial overachievement, the desire for perfectionism, and unending task-based motivation may end up as significant positive faculty traits as they try to create effective learning environments. While it is true that millennials assume their way is best, there is also an embedded willingness in millennials to learn, receive feedback, evolve and adapt. Their constant self-assessment and willingness to go beyond traditional classroom norms may end up changing the higher education classroom forever. With that said, institutions must harness this mentality. The ability to take concerns or reactions and apply them effectively in the classroom, or even in the institutional system at large, will not happen naturally. Institutions must consider how they onboard new faculty and, even more so, how they establish faculty and professional development opportunities.

References

Austin, A. E. (2002). Creating a bridge to the future: Preparing new faculty to face changing expectations in a shifting context. *The Review of Higher Education, 26*(2), 119-144.

Association of American Colleges & Universities, (2018, October 13). High-impact practices. Retrieved from https://www.aacu.org/resources/high-impact-practices

Bishop-Clark, C., & Dietz-Uhler, B. (2012). *Engaging the scholarship of teaching and learning: A guide to the process, and how to develop a project from start to finish.* Sterling, VA: Stylus.

Boyer, E. L. (1997). *Scholarship reconsidered: Priorities of the professoriate.* Princeton, N.J.: Carnegie Foundation for the Advancement of Teaching.

Brown, S. (2016, July 18). When millennials become managers. Retrieved from https://www.chronicle.com/article/When-Millennials-Become/237116

Brown, S. (2017, September 17). How generations X, Y and Z may change the academic workplace. Retrieved from https://www.chronicle.com/article/How-Generations-X-YZ-/241185

Cahill, T. F., & Sedrak, M. (2012). Leading a multigenerational workforce: strategies for attracting and retaining millennials. *Frontiers of Health Services Management, 29*(1), 3-15.

Evans, D. (2009, September 14). Redefining faculty roles. Retrieved from https://www.chronicle.com/blogs/onhiring/redefining-faculty-roles/8016

Friedman, J. (2018, January 11). Study: More students are enrolling in online courses. Retrieved from https://www.usnews.com/higher-education/online-education/articles/2018-01-11/study-more-students-are-enrolling-in-online-courses

Harrison, D. F. (2017, October 23). The role of higher education in the changing world of work. Retrieved from https://er.educause.edu/articles/2017/10/the-role-of-higher-education-in-the-changing-world-of-work

Kolb, D. A. (1984). *Experiential learning: Experience as the source of learning and development.* Englewood Cliffs, NJ: Prentice Hall.

Monzo, W. R., & Mitchell, K. M. W. (2018). We need to rethink training for Ph.D.s. Retrieved from https://www.insidehighered.com/advice/2018/09/11/academic-training-phds-needs-focus-more-teaching-opinion

Pedler, M. (2011). Leadership, risk and the imposter syndrome. *Action Learning: Research and Practice, 8*(2), 89–91. doi: 10.1080/14767333.2011.581016

Rikleen, L. S. (2012). Creating tomorrow's leaders: The expanding roles of Millennials in the workplace. *Boston College Center for Work and Family.* Retrieved from http://

www.bc.edu/content/dam/files/centers/cwf/research/publications/executivebriefing-series/Executive%20Briefing_Creating%20Tomorrows%20Leaders_Millennials

Sweet, C., Blythe, H., & Carpenter, R. (2016). *Innovating faculty development: Entering the age of innovation*. Stillwater, OK: New Forums Press.

Weimer, M. (2006). *Enhancing scholarly work on teaching and learning: Professional literature that makes a difference*. San Francisco, CA: Jossey-Bass.

Teaching and Learning Faculty Vignettes

Black Millennial Faculty Engaging Black Gen Z Students

Jasmin M. Goodman, Howard University, Fellow of Preparing Future Faculty (doctoral student)

Wei Sun, Howard University, Assistant Professor

The following paragraphs reflect a Black Millennial instructor's best practices in teaching Black Gen Z college students from a Historically Black College/University (HBCU). These include: lead with authenticity and respect; be mindful of culture and social justice; and be consistent with structure, interactivity, and accessibility.

1. Lead with Authenticity and Respect

As a Black Millennial instructor, my Netflix binges, social media use, and music interests tend to overlap with those of my students. Admittedly, while I cannot keep up with every social media trend or up-and-coming pop star, our interests align more often than not. Because I began teaching in higher education early in my career, I decided not to shy away from the closeness in age and fully embrace it. I found that embracing my love for popular culture, hip hop, social media, and all things Netflix has created more authentic interactions with my students. In short, Black Gen Z students value Black Millennial professors who show up as their authentic selves.

2. Be mindful of Culture and Social Justice

Teaching at a Historically Black College and University (HBCU) provides a unique opportunity when interacting with Gen Z students. In my experience teaching undergraduate-level public speaking courses, many students enter the University with a commitment to their culture, social justice issues, and activism. While the majority of students come from different socioeconomic, religious, and ethnic backgrounds—all of which must be respected. Many of the students desire to enter professions that will allow them to return to their communities and ignite change. I found it particularly helpful to leverage these interests during lectures and speech assignments. By using examples like actor Jesse Williams' 2016 *BET Awards* speech where he called for police reform and Beyonce's 2017 *Grammy* speech where she advocated for greater diversity in media representation, I was able to engage students in a lively discussion about the issues near to their hearts while relating it to course content.

3. Be consistent with Structure, Interactivity, and Accessibility

Black Gen Z students value a structured classroom, interactive assignments, and digital accessibility to their professors. In an attempt to liven up my teaching style a few semesters back, I transitioned away from traditional lecture presentations and incorporated more group activities and class discussions to foster a more engaging learning environment. While a few students enjoyed the experience, most students hated it and they vehemently expressed their frustrations on the end-of-course evaluation. Among the specific items they requested were more lectures and fewer in-class activities.

Students also appreciated the use of mobile communication apps like *Remind* which allow me to send text message blasts to my students. They can also use the app to send me quick messages if they were going to be late, or if they had questions about an upcoming deadline. As a note, the app allows you to set office hours so students know when to send messages and completely shields your phone number to keep your personal information private.

To meet the needs of the Millennial faculty population, it is important to lend these instructors the flexibility and resources to create engaging and authentic learning environments for their students.

Building Spaces for Millennial Faculty/ Student Engagement

Kevin Dvorak, Nova Southeastern University, Professor/ Executive Director, Writing & Communication Center

Walking around the developing downtown area(s) in the city where I live, Fort Lauderdale, it is fascinating to see the number of work places and work spaces that reflect millennial ideals, particularly in the number of intentional, shared co-working spaces. These work environments provide opportunities for individuals to rent work spaces for short periods of time, and they promote collaboration, community, engagement, and interaction in spaces that are often mostly open, with tables, wi-fi, and various technologies, with enclosed meeting areas adjacent to their larger open areas. These co-working facilities also often partner with a craft coffee maker or artisanal food group who provide energy to the people and space.

These types of third spaces—not quite home, not quite work—have long been found on university campuses in the form of writing/communication/teaching/learning centers. And, similar to their existence in downtown areas, writing and communication center are uniquely situated to provide millennial faculty with opportunities for collaboration and teamwork, flexible scheduling, feedback and communication, innovating with technology, and meaningful interaction.

These campus third spaces also allow millennial faculty to connect with students outside the classroom in ways that are meaningful to both parties. Over the course of the past year, as we have developed our new Writing and Communication Center, millennial faculty have used our space to

- host writing workshops for graduate students (that are available synchronously online);
- hold weekly "write-ins" for students and faculty working on larger projects, such as theses, dissertations, and manuscripts (also available online);
- facilitate faculty teaching workshops, primarily addressing topics related to student engagement;
- mentor graduate assistants who work in our center;
- mentor graduate and undergraduate peer writing and communication consultants

Our center is a space where millennial faculty gain experience working closely with students outside of class in an environment where power dynamics are lessened. For example, facilitating graduate student writing workshops allows our millennial faculty to develop teaching skills working with high level students across the entire university in areas such as health sciences, psychology, and engineering, rather than spending their years as a junior faculty member teaching first-year composition and/or undergraduate writing courses. It allows millennial faculty to develop close working partnerships with students who are relatively close in age (and are likely millennials themselves) in a workshop environment, where teamwork and collaboration are critical.

Another example of our third space in action is the "weekly write-in," which was designed to allow writers to meet together once a week to write for a few hours in a collaborative atmosphere. While this event takes place physically in our center, students are allowed to join online. We have cameras set up in our teaching and learning studio so that students who are at remote campuses, or just home with their families after a long day of work, can feel connected to our space and our community.

These are but a few examples for providing millennial faculty ways to use writing and communication center spaces to engage with students. Developing a workshop/event series provides millennials flexibility and entrepreneurial ownership, and using technology-based assessment tools (e.g., online surveys) at the end of each event can provide instant feedback on their performance. Being part of a writing and communication center also means being connected to something bigger than the classroom, namely the ability to make meaningful connections with—and having a positive impact on—an entire university's student population.

Section IV
The Faculty Transition

The process of onboarding new faculty has been discussed by faculty development scholars and researchers. On many campuses, this process involves a multi-day new faculty orientation experience. New faculty orientation programs usually take place on the ground, and involve a variety of informational experiences where faculty receive content focused on services and resources on campus. The onboarding process of new faculty is a critical moment for not only the faculty member but the academic institution. During this time, faculty transition to new roles, expectations, and workflows at the institution. Adjusting to a new academic institution can be exciting but also challenging for millennial faculty.

As Strawser and Hether (2019) explained:

> Because millennials are just now becoming fully integrated in the higher education culture as faculty and staff, rather than as students, the ramifications of how the typically rigid, top-down model will respond to millennials have yet to be fully understood. We do know that millennials possibly will challenge the status quo and may refuse to accept tradition as a valid excuse for present behavior. Therefore, it is important, generally, to understand how millennials engage in a professional environment and then apply these behaviors specifically to higher education. (pp. 1-2)

In this chapter, we address the primary considerations in the faculty transition. This chapter includes practical recommendations for supporting millennial faculty through the transition to a new campus. This chapter focuses on four areas, including:

- New faculty orientation and the faculty transition;
- Priorities for onboarding millennial faculty;
- New faculty orientation development process; and
- Millennial faculty success.

Think about it . . .

What might millennial faculty expect during their transition to a new institution? What might they expect in their first faculty role?

_____
_____
_____
_____
_____
_____
_____

What measures might higher education institutions take to ensure that new millennial faculty are welcome yet prepared?

_____
_____
_____
_____
_____
_____
_____

New Faculty Orientation and the Faculty Transition

New faculty orientation is an investment in the short- and long-term success of faculty members. Millennial faculty will require higher education institutions to adjust the onboarding process and experience. New faculty orientation is an opportunity to help new millennial faculty develop community on their new campus through collaborative experiences and engagement through technology (see Carpenter, 2019). The faculty transition can introduce multiple challenges to new faculty:

- Adjusting to teaching at the academic institution;
- Aligning teaching with scholarly and research expectations;
- Developing a scholarly agenda; and
- Assessing opportunities for academic service.

While new millennial faculty are often eager to begin their careers at their new institution, research suggests that they are also seeking rapid promotion and recognition (Ng, Schweitzer, & Lyons, 2010). As Strawser and Hether (2019) explained:

> The academy also provides extensive opportunities for individual recognition as well as collaboration. Publication, teaching and research awards, and grants are available from multiple sources and they all provide millennial faculty an ongoing opportunity for feedback and recognition. Faculty also receive feedback on their teaching at the end of every term in the form of course evaluations. Millennials'

team orientation, on the other hand, is supported through committee work as well as participation in collaborative research and writing projects, as well as co-teaching opportunities. (p. 15)

Priorities for Onboarding Millennial Faculty

Millennial faculty members are achievement oriented and connected to the world as well as their institutions. Bucalos and Strawser (2017) argued that "[t]he opportunity to describe millennials, especially millennial faculty members, is continually relevant" (p. 19). Given these questions, Bucalos and Strawser investigated how this generation of faculty will respond to the structure and system of higher education institutions. They continue by explaining that as more millennials assume faculty roles, higher education institutions must respond and meet their needs.

Millennial faculty face unique challenges as they navigate the professional college network from first year to tenure and beyond.

Think about it . . .

What priorities would you list for supporting millennial faculty with the transition to a new campus or faculty role?

_____

_____

_____

_____

_____

_____

_____

_____

What resources might new millennial faculty expect or need?

_____

_____

_____

_____

_____

_____

_____

New Faculty Orientation Development Process

New faculty orientation will likely be the faculty member's primary introduction to the campus and its faculty. The new faculty orientation experience sets the tone for the faculty life cycle. While many orientations are designed to deliver information, new millennial faculty will expect opportunities to learn in ways that they find most productive and effective. Millennials appreciate collaborative or team experiences. This characteristic is critical to the design of new faculty orientation and related faculty development experiences for new faculty. At this event, new faculty learn about teaching and learning philosophies endorsed by the higher education campus they are now joining. In addition, promotion and tenure policies and timelines are shared during the early days on the new faculty orientation experience and can be aligned with faculty development requirements or opportunities, scholarly priorities, and mentoring protocol. While many new faculty orientation programs are designed to simply introduce new faculty to operational units of the institution such as human resources, parking, or on-campus dining, the program at Eastern Kentucky University is designed as interactive, valuing faculty learning. Many faculty development programs involve initiatives that focus on honing skills such as leadership (Sweet, Blythe, & Carpenter, 2018; Sweet, Blythe, Phillips, & Carpenter, 2018; DeZure, Shaw, & Rojewski, 2014).

How would you design a new faculty orientation experience for a millennial faculty member?

_____
_____
_____
_____
_____
_____

How might you revise current or traditional new faculty orientation programming to reach millennial faculty?

_____
_____
_____
_____
_____
_____

Millennial Faculty Success

Millennial faculty success will likely be determined by advancement through the promotion and tenure process. Activities that are rewarded during this timeframe, often the first five to six years as a tenure-track assistant professor, are often assessed by scholarship, teaching, and service. Depending on the institution's classification, faculty seeking promotion may be asked to demonstrate contributions to the field, including national recognition.

The millennial faculty member will determine success not only by goals and achievements but also through experiences and interactions beginning with new faculty orientation. The new faculty orientation experience should account for several expectations millennial expectations:

- Rapid information and distillation;
- Lack of social distinctions;

- Motivation by purpose, academic mission, and skill over time in rank or traditional advancement processes;
- Opportunities for early advancement based on vision and deliverables; and
- Instant responses.

What is Millennial Faculty Success?

Risk taking, responsibility, and grit will look different for millennials. New millennial faculty will need to be supported as they transition to teaching, scholarship, and service at the institution. Table 1 outlines the millennial faculty process, which includes aspects of faculty expectations (or faculty criteria) and the millennial process that can allow for development.

Table 1. Millennial Faculty Processes

Faculty Criteria	Millennial Process
Scholarship	Collaboration Mentorship Immediate Feedback
Teaching	Technology and media Social media
Service	Belief in mission Supportive of goals
Faculty Development	Related to advancement Perpetually available

Think about it . . .

How would you define millennial faculty success?

_____

_____

_____

_____

_____

How might millennial faculty define success?

_____

_____

What Faculty Transition Programs Can and Should Do

Faculty transition programs are crucial at any academic institution. What can and should they do to support faculty success?

Table 2. Faculty Transition Support

Faculty Transition Program	Support Rationale
New Faculty Orientation	New Faculty Orientation establishes a foundation for faculty culture at the institution. Usually lasting three to four days, New Faculty Orientation allows faculty an introduction to the institution while also the opportunity to collaborate with faculty from across campus. Faculty learn the basic information about the institution at New Faculty Orientation.
Faculty Mentor Program	Faculty mentor programs allow new millennial faculty to build relationships within and beyond their academic departments. Relationships built in a faculty mentor program can help faculty acclimate to the expectations of the institution.
Online Faculty Development	Online options can leverage technology to ensure that new millennial faculty have access to teaching and learning support at any time. Use of badging and social media can also enhance engagement (see Sweet, Blythe, Carpenter, & Cecil, 2018; Carpenter, 2017.
Scholarship Academy	A Scholarship Academy can help support new millennial faculty as they adjust to the research and scholarship expectations of their institution. In addition, these experiences allow millennial faculty to identify and build faculty collaborative teams.

As indicated by Table 2, strategies for supporting the millennial faculty transition can be refined to acknowledge the preferences of millennial faculty (see Smith & Nichols, 2015).

Think about it . . .

What other support might millennial faculty expect, need, or benefit from?

_____

_____

_____

_____

_____

Can you add programs to Table 2? If so, what would you add and why?

_____

_____

_____

_____

Setting up Faculty Teams

Moore and Vincent (2019) explained, "the generational characteristics of millennials are reshaping how millennial faculty think about academic scholarship" (p. 94). Millennial faculty prefer working collaboratively in teams. What are the key considerations that factor in the design of millennial faculty teams?

Table 3. Millennial Faculty Teams

Strategy	Rationale
Offer personalized, individualized faculty development.	Help millennial faculty see connection to faculty collaborators that spans career and lifestyle.
Employ technology and media in the design of faculty development.	Encourage faculty to support one another through the formation of online, mediated teams or groups.
Recognize team-based teaching, scholarship and service.	Millennial faculty form and function collaboratively. Acknowledging collaborative work can serve as a retention and growth strategy.

As Table 3 suggests, higher education institutions can design strategies for ensuring faculty success inside and outside of the classroom, in common areas used to evaluate for promotion and tenure. For millennial faculty, this process will:

- Show a commitment to their learning and success;
- Promote relationships inside and outside of the department that can yield meaningful relationships;
- Allow for the formation of productive partnerships as they pursue promotion and tenure;
- Establish the academic institution as a space where they are supported, that is responsive to the working environments of millennial faculty; and
- Promote faculty productivity.

What is missing in much of the discussion of productive faculty teams is an examination of the value placed on faculty leadership. On our own campuses, faculty leadership development is prioritized among the development opportunities available. At Eastern Kentucky University, for example, faculty can participate in the annual Faculty Leadership Institute (FLI), which is organized through the Faculty Center for Teaching & Learning (FCT&L) and Noel Studio for Academic Creativity. At the University of Central Florida (UCF), a research one university situated in Orlando, FL, the Academic Leadership Academy cultivates leadership skills across departments and colleges. These experiences are intended for faculty to build the skills they need to serve on (and lead) university committees and to pursue other forms of leadership such as program coordinator or department chair. At EKU, though, working collaboratively in teams is a component of the faculty leadership development experience. Using tools such as the Five Paths to Leadership, by Academic Impressions, faculty explore skills they can develop early on in their careers to prepare them for committee and leadership work in ensuing years.

How might millennial faculty design teams to support or advance their academic work?

_____

_____

_____

_____

_____

_____

How would you describe an effective team? How might millennial faculty?

_____

_____

_____

_____

_____

Collaboration

While collaboration is often discussed within the context of the professoriate, it warrants more attention when discussing faculty development designed for millennials. Millennials will expect collaborative environments and institutions that recognize and facilitate collaborative efforts. Higher education institutions can support millennial faculty by creating experiences that allow them to explore and learn best practices for collaboration. Millennial faculty will expect supportive collaborative relationships and facilitation of these experiences through faculty development. These faculty development experiences might include those in areas of research and teaching.

Collaboration will be critical to a millennial faculty member's success across institutional classifications and goals. However, as faculty transition into their new roles, faculty development experiences can model to new faculty ways in which collaborative experiences can be most beneficial and productive in pursuing academic goals.

Why might collaborative opportunities be important to new millennial faculty during their transition to a new campus?

_____

_____

_____

_____

_____

What challenges might new millennial faculty face in designing collaborations?

_____

_____

_____

_____

_____

Research

Millennial faculty will anticipate academic institutions that are responsive to collaborative relationships and the development of collaborative cultures of scholarship, research, and creative endeavors. New Faculty Orientation and professional development programs designed for new faculty can highlight collaborative opportunities. Moreover, cluster-hire initiatives—those faculty hires focused on recruiting faculty from diverse disciplines as productive research teams—must be supported long after they are recruited to campus. To support new millennial faculty in the transition, orientations can:

- Offer strategies for forming effective collaborative working teams in areas of research and publishing;
- Provide approaches to forming new research collaborations, including establishing agreed-upon expectations;
- Share best practices for establishing timelines for research projects; and
- Explain how to establish new scholarly research proj-

ects—including those focused on teaching and learning—to enhance research and student learning.

In this process, faculty transitions can involve, as Smith (2019) suggested, mentoring, collaboration, and guidelines for success and feedback.

Think about it . . .

Explore ways in which millennial faculty might expect to establish productive research collaborations.

_____

_____

_____

_____

_____

What can faculty development programs do to support new millennial faculty in designing and managing research collaborations?

_____

_____

_____

_____

_____

Teaching

New faculty orientation—and first-year faculty programs—can support and promote collaborative approaches to teaching. While co-taught courses are often a possibility at academic institutions, it is not always possible to place these courses on the schedule each semester or to offer these opportunities to all faculty. Thus, academic institutions might coordinate collaborative teaching experiences in the form of teaching observations, guest presentations, and content-area focused workshops, at times through the teaching and learning center.

Millennial faculty will anticipate—and expect—opportunities for networking while preparing for teaching assignments and honing teaching skills. Faculty development can factor as a centralizing opportunity that aligns millennial faculty with the institution and other faculty. Therefore, faculty development related to teaching can provide social engagement as well as practical strategies to enhance this area of the professoriate. Within faculty development units on campuses, however, mentoring can build community and encourage retention among millennial faculty. Often assigned during—or just after—new faculty orientation, mentoring programs can be critical to faculty success in teaching (see Bland et al., 2009; Conway, 2018; Johnson & Ridley, 2018; Meschitti & Smith, 2017; Mylona, 2016; Phillips & Dennison, 2015).

As mentioned previously, scholarship of teaching and learning (SoTL) research can also provide opportunities for millennial faculty as they transition to the institution.

Think about it . . .

What will new millennial faculty expect when planning to teach?

_____

_____

_____

_____

_____

Based on available research, how might millennial faculty approach their teaching during the first year at a new institution?

_____

_____

_____

_____

_____

Scholarship

As Gardner (2016) explained, millennial faculty are highly collaborative, and this expectation transfers to scholarly approaches. This attribute will impact the ways millennial faculty navigate scholarly processes, including publishing and presenting their work, two of the most common forms of academic exchanges. Higher education institutions will need to prepare millennial faculty for navigating publication and presentation challenges and opportunities. As Sweet, Blythe, Phillips, and Carpenter (2017) have examined, all faculty need guidance and support in the publication process. Millennial faculty will need mentoring focused on prioritizing and evaluating authorship. While many institutions still prioritize single-authored work, others support collaborative research and scholarship. Millennial faculty will require clear guidelines on scholarly requirements, and these will need to be established from the beginning, likely in new faculty orientation, as well as being reinforced by the deans and department chairs. A responsiveness to collaborative opportunities will encourage millennial faculty to thrive in the higher education environment. Research design and publications or presentations coauthored by multiple authors will be preferable to millennial scholars. Moreover, scholarship that is both research and development (design) driven will allow millennial new faculty important opportunities that resonate with their own value structures.

For one recent strategy that will resonate with millennial faculty members, see the University of Michigan's Paper Sprint (Ryan, Kerppola, & Verhey-Henke, n.d.). The paper sprint, as the authors explain, is a highly productive and collaborative process wherein each member of the authorship and research team plays a role to allow for maximum productivity. What will resonate with the millennial faculty member, though, is the focus on the following:

- team-based authorship,
- collaboration,
- productivity, and
- recognition.

Producing scholarship can present challenges. How would you mentor a millennial faculty member to produce scholarship?

_____

_____

_____

_____

_____

What approaches might be most successful for millennial faculty when designing scholarly projects?

_____

_____

_____

_____

_____

Strategies

- Review new faculty orientation schedules for opportunities to incorporate collaboration and to design lasting relationship for and with millennial new faculty.
- Establish mentoring opportunities that extend beyond new faculty orientation.
- Encourage 21st-century innovation among new faculty members and provide multiple paths toward meaningful scholarship.
- Productively disrupt traditional leadership and scholarly dynamics.
- Encourage meaningful participation in scholarship of teaching and learning (SoTL).
- Design interactive experiences for new faculty that will encourage team building and collaboration inside and outside of the departmental structure.

Questions

- In what ways does your academic institution's new faculty orientation promote strategies for success among millennial faculty?
- How might you make the first-year experience at your campus more engaging for millennial new faculty?
- What attributes might a new faculty mentoring process involve to best support millennial faculty?
- In what ways might current faculty development practices need to be adjusted to meet expectations and needs of new millennial faculty?

Think about it . . .

What lessons learned from the millennial faculty transition are most prominent?

_____

_____

_____

_____

_____

How will you plan (or plan differently) as you plan for millennial faculty on your own campus?

_____

_____

_____

_____

_____

What programming will you design or update based on available research on millennial faculty?

_____

_____

_____

_____

_____

References

Bland, C. J., Taylor, A. L., Shollen, L., Weber-Main, A. M., & Mulcahy, P. A. (2009). *Faculty success through mentoring: A guide for mentors, mentees, and leaders.* Lanham, MD: Rowman & Littlefield.

Bucalos, A., & Strawser, M. (2017). Mentoring millennial faculty. *2017 Proceedings IU Southeast Scholarship of Teaching and Learning Conference.* 19-25.

Carpenter, R. (2019). Faculty development and millennial faculty. In M. Strawser (Ed.), *Leading millennial faculty: Navigating the new professoriate* (pp. 147-166). Lanham, MD: Lexington Books.

Carpenter, R. (2017). Faculty development in the digital age: Training instructors in new media pedagogy. In M. Strawser (Ed.), *New media and digital pedagogy: Enhancing the twenty-first century classroom* (pp. 55–78). Lanham, MD: Lexington Books.

Conway, C. S., ed. (2018). *Faculty mentorship at historically black colleges and universities.* Hershey, PA: IGI Global.

DeZure, D., Shaw, A., & Rojewski, J. (2014). Cultivating the Next Generation of Academic Leaders: Implications for Administrators and Faculty. *Change: The Magazine of Higher Learning. 46,* 6-12.

Gardner, S. K. (2016). Mentoring the millennial faculty member. *The Department Chair: A Resource for Academic Administrators, 27*(1), 6-8.

Johnson, W. B., & Ridley, C. R. (2018). *The elements of mentoring.* New York, NY: St. Martin's Press.

Meschitti, V., & Smith, H. L. (2017). Does mentoring make a difference for women in academics? Evidence from the literature and a guide for future research. *Journal of Research in Gender Studies, 7*(1), 166-199.

Mylona, E., Brubaker, L., Williams, V. N., Novielli, K. D., Lyness, J. M., Pollart, S. M., Dandar, V., & Bunton, S. A. (2016). Does formal mentoring for faculty members matter? A survey of clinical faculty members. *Medical Education, 50,* 670-681.

Ng, E. S., Schweitzer, L., & Lyons, S. T. (2010). New generation, great expectations: A field study of the millennial generation. *Journal of Business and Psychology,* 25(2), 281-292.

Phillips, S. L., & Dennison, S. T. (2015). *Faculty mentoring: A practical manual for mentors, mentees, administrators, and faculty developers.* Sterling, VA: Stylus.

Ryan, A., Kerppola, M. & Verhey-Henke, A. (n.d.). *How to conduct paper sprints.* Retrieved from file:///Users/deployeduser/Downloads/Paper_Sprint_Manual%20(3).pdf

Smith, S. (2019). Millennial faculty expectations of communication. In M. Strawser (Ed.), *Leading millennial faculty: Navigating the new professoriate* (pp. 73-86). Lanham, MD: Lexington Books.

Smith, T. J., & Nichols, T. (2015). Understanding the millennial generation. *Journal of Business Diversity, 15*(1), 39-47.

Strawser, M. & Hether, H. (2019). The millennial faculty invasion. In M. Strawser (Ed.), *Leading millennial faculty: Navigating the new professoriate* (pp. 1-14). Lanham, MD: Lexington Books.

Sweet, C., Blythe, H., & Carpenter, R. (2018). Innovating academic leadership. *National Teaching and Learning Forum, 27*(3), 9-11.

Sweet, C., Blythe, H., Carpenter, R., & Cecil, T. (2018). Approaching the Holy Grail of faculty development: Evolving a CTL from a service-oriented organization to a learning-assessment unit. *Journal on Centers for Teaching and Learning, 10,* 45-58

Sweet, C., Blythe, H., Phillips, B., & Carpenter, R. (2018). *Ten habits of innovative leaders: Executing a game plan for academic leadership.* Stillwater, OK: New Forums Press.

The Faculty Transition Faculty Vignettes

Welcoming and Supporting Millennial Faculty

Sara L. Zeigler, Eastern Kentucky University, Dean and Professor, College of Letters, Arts, and Social Sciences

Having recently reached my 20-year milestone in my post-doctoral life as an academician and my fifteenth year in administration, I have experienced the privilege and pain of observing and adapting to generational changes among both students and faculty. Our focus tends to be on students, but the need to shape a workplace that can support, encourage, and develop new faculty is critical.

When I arrived at EKU, most of my colleagues were baby boomers – I was the outlier, as a Gen X faculty member who preferred email (how very quaint!) to meetings, preferred to write from the library or from home, and who would eagerly take on more work to avoid having a committee do it instead. I had many things in common with my colleagues – I would do more than was asked of me, did not expect my job to be clearly defined, and actually preferred (and still prefer) ambiguity so that I could define my own goals, priorities, and interests, within the context of institutional and student needs.

As I moved into the role of academic dean responsible for faculty development and university-wide curricular work in 2010 and then into a very traditional college dean role in 2016, I noticed shifts in the needs of my faculty. Like my generation, the millennial faculty do not want to be tied to the workplace, but prefer to work remotely, choosing the spaces and hours that make them most productive. They are even more comfortable and adept with technology and have pushed me to adopt Google docs, texting, and messaging to replace more conventional forms of collaboration and communication. All of that is energizing and encouraging.

The transformation that has given me the greatest pause – and the greatest need to adapt – has been the need for sharply written, well-defined professional expectations. For this group of faculty, I must lay out the demands of the job with surprising specificity – with clarity that borders on harshness. Over the last year, I have found myself creating strict professional development plans to address what I perceived as an unwillingness to be good college citizens. My chairs report similar challenges. We now tell faculty members that they are required to hold office hours and tell them exactly how many – and that being available by text or email is insufficient. I have had to inform faculty members that they should not raise their voices in meetings or to their department chairs (their supervisors!) and have had faculty members tell me, with all sincerity, that they did not intend to offend or be defiant. They simply did not see the behavior as disrespectful. For the first time, when I met with my newly hired faculty, I told them that neglecting to pursue professional development in the area of pedagogy would adversely affect their chances for reappointment – in past years, I could "strongly encourage" such action and faculty would eagerly attend sessions.

The millennial faculty are energetic, technologically savvy, and willing to experiment with their pedagogy. However, they bring a new culture with them and I am changing my practices accordingly. To my fellow aging deans, I suggest the following:

- *Articulate expectations clearly, bluntly, and in written form, with consequences clearly defined*: Millennial faculty will do the work, but will not take a suggestion as a directive. If there are neither consequences nor rewards, they will follow their own inclinations.

- *Provide professional development opportunities that are flexible and incorporate technology*: Allow for self-paced work that can be done at any hour, asynchronous collaboration, and choice of topic – the faculty will seek out the support when a problem arises and they will want immediate access.
- *Communicate frequently and clearly*: All faculty like to know about key institutional changes, but millennial faculty demand more frequent contact and more specificity.
- *Offer prompt feedback, without sugar-coating*: When a millennial faculty member is off track, a quick, stern correction is often sufficient to produce the desired change.

Welcoming New Faculty Into a Changing Community

Anne B. Bucalos, Bellarmine University, Professor of Education and Vice Provost for Faculty Development

What has changed from past practices in mentoring and orienting new faculty as they transition into either higher education, a specific institution, or both? In one word, "everything!" Having just completed a two-day, whole group mentoring/orientation program for our newest faculty at my university – which is just the beginning of two intensive mentoring/orientation programs for new colleagues that will move them through their first year – I can say that both the content and focus have changed dramatically, even from five years ago. In addition to the increased duration of mentoring and orientation programming to a full year, cross-disciplinary mentoring teams have been implemented to encourage collaboration, creativity, and community-building. Five years ago the emphasis was on "How do you fit into our university in order to be successful," to this year's "What is the changing role of faculty as key partners in student retention and success?" In the past, new faculty mentoring was individualized, within the context of helping each colleague be successful in teaching, scholarship and service. Mentors were guides to full entry into the institution.

A quick glance at the recent agenda for the 2018-19 initial whole group orientation session says it all: topics ranged from testing accommodations for students with disabilities, to handling Title IX sexual misconduct violations, to assisting transgender students who are transitioning with registering their chosen name on class rosters. Yes, there was still a bit of university history and sharing of research interests, but there was considerably more content on usage of our complex campus information systems and how to "file" a FIRE report on a student who may need early professional intervention from our "CARE" team.

What does this mean for our newest faculty colleagues, especially millennial faculty who are coming out of their doctoral programs or from the private sector? Is their perception of the faculty role any different from their more senior colleagues? Have their graduate programs prepared them for the shift from "sage on the stage" to their very significant role in the retention of students? As lovers of everything technological, do they know the intricacies of successfully integrating tech strategies into their teaching? As a generation more accustomed to diversity, do they understand assistance animal policies and what it means to work with students who use a screen reader? And, as they work on their scholarly agendas, does their propensity for collaboration find its way into the kind of community-based scholarship of teaching and learning that most benefits students' success? Faculty developers must address the characteristics unique to millennial faculty and their mentoring needs, especially if we want to retain them as happy, successful professionals.

However higher education, and especially private liberal arts institutions, will survive only if collectively we acknowledge the expanding roles of faculty, mentoring them as they develop a new skill set for effectively working with students of today and the future. Millennial faculty are poised to use their desires for collaboration, flexibility, continuous communication, and results-oriented feedback to effect the kind of change that will enhance the experiences of students, while also contributing to new communities of possibility for faculty and staff. Mentoring not just "to fit," but "to shape" will be a key component of their success as faculty, their students' success as learners, and the survival of their institutions.

What do we learn as we embrace millennial faculty as integral colleagues in this rapidly changing venue of higher education? A few points to note:

- Mentoring should not be localized exclusively within a department, or even an orchestrated pairing. It is most effective in cross-generational and cross-disciplinary groups, where new faculty and more senior colleagues come together with various perspectives and histories of institutional culture, sharing both "how it has been done," and "how it could be done."

- Diversity (age, gender, race, etc.) is key in forming mentoring groups, especially in fostering relationships and combating social isolation. This is especially important for new, often millennial faculty who may have moved from another state or country and/or are individuals from less represented groups on campus.

- Multiage mentoring, especially in groups, facilitates a collaborative ethos on a campus that can encourage cooperative scholarship endeavors, peer review of teaching that is less evaluative and more developmental (apart from a department chair's), and mutual sharing of different skill sets – addressing the needs of many millennials.

- Whole group orienting of new faculty, especially millennials, provides a consistent message of expectations within a context of non-evaluation (we are all new, so there's no silly question), and with a supportive structure around accepted processes and procedures on a given campus. Campus "myths" can be addressed, as can appropriate avenues for requests, complaints, and questions about advancement, protocol, and responsibilities.

Thus, when a millennial faculty wants to know why she can't go up for tenure after two years instead of six, or why a department chair can't just remove that "unruly" student from his class, or even why they have to be on campus during "office hours" instead of handling them electronically, there are networks of colleagues with whom to engage for answers and feedback.

Mentoring Millennials is Not for Administrators

Donna M. Elkins, Spalding University, Communication

One of many benefits I uncovered after moving from a senior level administrative position in a large community college to a full-time faculty position in a small liberal arts university was that of being able to be a mentor for younger faculty. It's not that I did not want to do this in my previous role. When I was an academic dean, I took notice of new millennial hires in whom I saw potential. I would request they sit on certain committees, arrange chats just to see how they were doing, or offer advice about the promotion and evaluation process. Even though I had greatly valued this type of personal opportunity with leaders when I began my career and saw those leaders as important mentors, none of these relationships with millennials ever seemed to move beyond the supervisor-subordinate role.

I was disappointed, because from my perspective senior level administrators were best placed to be mentors to the incoming millennial workforce. But I also knew that these types of relationships need to develop and grow organically, so I put it down to just not being the right person for those particular new members of our institution. However, when I decided to step out of administration and took a role as a full professor in a small liberal arts university, my perception about administrative mentors changed quickly.

After a year of being the new person myself and learning the new political and cultural climates on my campus, I realized that other younger women on the faculty and staff were often seeking me out, not for the types of questions I had previously fielded as an administrator about rules and regulations, but for advice on conflict, encouragement after a disappointing class, decisions about which committees to join, just to have lunch, or to talk about overall philosophies of teaching and education. As time went on, even some millennial staff members from my previous institution contacted me to talk about issues or decisions they were facing and to seek out encouragement for their career progress.

I have not changed my relational strategies or my openness to these types of relationships. What has changed? My role in the institution. In my experience millennial newcomers do not form or seek out mentoring relationships as easily with those in authority as with those who are experienced, but also "one of them."

My conclusion is that institutions would do well to consider three best practices if mentoring of millennial faculty is an important goal: (1) Do not just assign administrators (chairs, directors or deans) to be the "go to" person for new faculty, instead find seasoned professors or experienced colleagues and encourage them to fill that role for millennial faculty members; (2) Do not just assume new millennials will find their own mentor, instead be intentional about setting up opportunities for them to interact with experienced institutional members; and (3) Allow these relationships to develop organically, they either will or will not and that is dependent on the individuals involved, but forcing the relationship is generally not helpful.

Myths of Mentorship for Millennial Faculty Members

Stephanie A. Smith, Virginia Tech, Communication

I am more than halfway to tenure at a research-centric university and yet my feelings of panic, anxiety, and uncertainty remain high. However, because of the relationships I have formed with my peers and senior colleagues that I begin each semester with a renewed sense of optimism and opportunity. When I look back on my past three years, I realize how each moment, even the seemingly insignificant or vapid, led me into my next project, collaboration, or service opportunity. Without these friendships,

I'm scared to think of where I would be and how I would be feeling today. Although I have peers and senior colleagues that have been extremely gracious with their time, expertise, and support, I do not have a mentor. This is actually something I rarely admit since it seems like a big academic sin, especially for a woman.

I did receive a small grant from my college during my first year that could be used to develop a mentor/mentee relationship, but with someone outside of my particular institution, rather than within it. I, however, used this money to obtain a highly recommended certification which helped me meet several key players, but did not help me gain a mentor. Money is not the key to mentoring. Instead, I suggest a non-traditional approach to mentoring millennials in higher education.

First, millennial academics should be encouraged to have multiple mentors, rather than one. Perhaps more importantly, these relationships should be cultivated organically and not assigned or mandated. Sometimes, realizing you have multiple mentors is as easy as a shift in thinking about relationships. While I do not have one mentor, I do have specific people that I turn to for help. Some are best for professional advice, brainstorming, methodological help, and others just for commiserating. By these standards, each one of these people is a mentor, but none are my exclusive mentor.

This leads me to my second point about mentoring being a misconception. It is unrealistic to presume that one person can help with everything whenever you need it. Mentoring should be mutually beneficial for the mentor and the mentee, which is especially important to millennials. Understanding that millennials can teach more senior faculty just as much as they can learn from them changes the mentoring relationship entirely. However, it is possible to be a successful millennial academic without a mentor, and if mentorship is a point of stress, it should be reconsidered.

Finally, rather than pressuring pre-tenure faculty into forced relationships in an unfamiliar and often intimidating environment, millennial faculty should be encouraged to build their network. This will provide millennials with the freedom and flexibility they crave, but also lead to more lasting and valuable relationships in the future. This can be done through providing travel resources, helping connect faculty members with similar interests across departments and institutions, and by taking an active interest in the lives and work of millennial faculty members.

Section V
Millennial-Focused Faculty Development Programs

Millennial-Focused Faculty Development

Millennial faculty development programs can take many forms, yet are currently under-examined and lightly theorized. Much remains to be learned, tested, and assessed in this area in the coming years as millennial faculty enter campuses throughout the country and beyond.

This chapter focuses on millennial-focused faculty development programs. Moreover, this chapter will offer practical strategies and opportunities for reflection focused on millennial faculty development programs. We offer opportunities for reflection throughout the chapter as you consider options that transfer to your own campus contexts.

Let's begin with several questions focused on faculty development positioning on your home campus.

1. What faculty development opportunities are offered on your home campus?
2. To what extent have you discussed millennial faculty with colleagues or members of your faculty development program?

As Kelly (2009) explained, it is important to consider millennial faculty before they arrive on campus because planning will take years to design and implement. Millennials desire a purposeful work experience. Thus, it is important to treat them as individuals and to personalize faculty development opportunities. Millennials are driven by career advancement. Participation in faculty development is a path toward advancement, especially in teaching and scholarship, two pillars often used to assess faculty success. Faculty development programs for millennials must be:

- Purposeful
- Personalized
- Engaging
- Involve current literature on faculty development programs
- Include literature on programs for millennials
- Evaluation

Comparing Faculty Development Programs and Millennial Faculty Development Programs

Faculty Development Programs	Millennial Faculty Development Programs
Ask faculty to come to them	Go to faculty where they are
Often in person	Often available in multiple forms
Focused on program priorities	Focused on faculty priorities

Take a few minutes to complete the inventory in Table 5.

Table 5. Faculty Development Inventory

Current Faculty Development Programs	Opportunities to Update or Shape Millennial Faculty Development Programs

What are the characteristics of millennial faculty development?

_____

_____

_____

_____

What to Avoid

- Dated topics
- Impractical topics

What to Embrace

As you design millennial-focused faculty development programs, consider ways in which the following can be incorporated (Drawing from Waljee, Chopra, & Saint, 2018).

- Innovation
- Autonomy
- Purpose
- Leadership
- Diversity
- Community

Design and Vision

- Audience
- Menu-driven Format
- Faculty Awards and Recognition

Implementation

- Communication
- Material
- Facilitators

Evaluation and Assessment

- Connection between millennial faculty, department, college, and institution

Sustainability

- Ways program can be developed in future semesters or years

Reflect

Use Table 6 to draft responses and notes focused on millennial faculty development programming.

Table 6. Millennial Faculty Development Attributes

Attribute	Millennial Faculty Development Programming
Innovation	
Purpose	
Leadership	
Diversity	
Community	
Audience	
Format	

Recognition	
Communication	
Facilitators	
Sustainability	

In Table 7, consider ways in which your faculty development programming can intentionally connect millennial faculty at each level.

Table 7. Connecting Millennial Faculty

Level	Strategies for Connecting Millennial Faculty
Center for Teaching & Learning	
Department	

College	
Institution	

At every level, connections to and for new millennial faculty are crucial to successful practices. Technology—in many forms—can allow for regular and efficient communication, a process of connecting millennial faculty with resources, people, and programs. Consider options for employing technology to engage millennial faculty in Table 8.

Table 8. Use of Technology

Technology	Description	Rationale	Millennial engagement outcome
Email			
Website			
Social Media			

Video			

Table 9. Technology Brainstorm

Technology	Description	Rationale	Millennial engagement outcome

What follows are strategies for engaging millennial faculty through faculty development programs that are commonly designed and implemented at higher education institutions of a variety of sizes and contexts.

Faculty development programs can be designed for formal and informal settings. Much of the work of faculty development is integrating relationship building with content focused on areas of the professoriate such as teaching, scholarship, and service.

Formal programs can be designed to serve a multitude of purposes, including:
- New faculty orientation
- Promotion and tenure processes
- Annual review

Informal faculty development programs can include:
- Faculty mentoring
- Lunch and learn (topical faculty development)
- Teaching circles (focused on issues and considerations related to teaching and learning)

Think about it . . .

What formal faculty development programs do you currently offer on your campus?

_____

_____

_____

_____

_____

What faculty development programs do you currently offer on your campus?

_____

_____

_____

_____

_____

How might formal faculty development programs be designed for millennial faculty?

_____

_____

_____

_____

_____

How might informal faculty development programs be designed for millennial faculty?

_____

_____

_____

_____

_____

How can formal and informal networks (digital and in person) be established to engage millennial faculty?

_____

_____

_____

_____

_____

References

Waljee, J.F., Chopra, V., & Saint, S. (2018). Mentoring millennials. *JAMA, 319(*15), 1547-1548.

Designing Engaging Workshops

Millennial faculty will expect high levels of interpersonal relationship building. Workshops can adhere to several criteria to engage millennial faculty (Table 10). Workshops are a common form of faculty development programs, especially focused on teaching and student learning.

Table 10. Millennial Faculty Engagement in Workshops

Workshop Content	Engagement Strategy	Outcome
Teaching and learning	Practice teaching and learning techniques Explore evidence from teaching and learning research and scholarship of teaching and learning (SoTL)	Millennial faculty experience teaching techniques that can be implemented in the classroom in formal or informal ways
Mentorship	Explore strategies for formal and informal mentoring Shadow mentors through programs or initiatives that allow faculty to see behind-the-scenes	Millennial faculty gather perspectives from mentors and mentees Millennial faculty experience the day-to-day work of leaders, administrators, and other faculty
Scholarship	Analyze scholarly models Discuss collaborative approaches for producing scholarship Hear from accomplished faculty researchers who can provide practical insight into processes	Millennial faculty follow the approaches and practices of successful teacher-scholars (Kuh, 2007)

Encouraging Millennial Faculty to "Buy-In" to Faculty Development

Millennial faculty will need help buying into faculty development programming. While some faculty will have experience with faculty development programs, others will likely be approaching programming for the first time (or will need support acclimating to new expectations). Buy in can be accomplished in multiple ways:

- High-quality opportunities
- Timely topics
- Collaborative opportunities that span disciplinary boundaries
- Regular communication
- Opportunities for advancement

Improving the Millennial Instructor's Teaching Skills

Millennial faculty are driven and have goals of being successful and pursuing advancement. Teaching is central to faculty success at many higher education institutions. While millennial faculty will likely bring to campus a variety of practices, the first and second year as a teaching faculty member can promote successful teaching practices (and help navigate those that might be less successful).

Consider these questions as you design teaching-focused faculty development for millennials:

- What research is available on this teaching strategy?
- What are the most effective ways to communicate (and teach) this approach?
- How will millennial faculty access and retain teaching content?

Think about it . . .

Efforts to improve teaching take place on a regular basis. What recommendations would you have for millennial faculty to improve teaching skills?

_____

_____

_____

_____

_____

In what ways would you recommend new millennial faculty reflect on their own teaching improvement efforts?

_____

_____

_____

_____

_____

What resources would you recommend new millennial faculty explore or pursue on your campus that might promote teaching improvement? How often might millennial faculty incorporate these resources and on what timeline during the academic year or semester?

_____

_____

_____

_____

_____

Understanding Course and Curriculum Design

Centers for teaching and learning, often referred to as CTLs, can be an ideal space on higher education campuses for millennial faculty to explore course design and curriculum (see Tassoni, 2009; Clark & Saulnier, 2010; Sweet, Blythe, Carpenter, & Cecil, 2018). While these topics are often explored as part of a CTL's annual programming, at some institutions they will need to seek this information elsewhere—sometimes at the department or college level and, in other cases, as part of online course design initiatives.

Millennial faculty can participate in course design initiatives that incorporate:

- Pre-semester strategies for designing, revising, or updating syllabi;
- Resources focused on current syllabus requirements;
- Models for incorporating active-learning strategies;

- Opportunities to consult with tenure or experienced faculty.

However, curriculum design might focus on:
- Alignment with departmental, college, or institutional goals;
- Drafting learning outcomes;
- Assuring student learning.

Think about it...

Where does curriculum development take place at your academic institution?

_____

_____

_____

_____

_____

How might the current (or future) infrastructures in place at your academic institution support course or curriculum development for millennial faculty?

_____

_____

_____

_____

_____

Explaining Assessment to Generation Y

Assessment is not often seen as every faculty member's job. Often we see it as something that takes place in a distant office somewhere on campus. Assessment, though, can be viewed by millennial faculty as an opportunity for continuous learning and improvement. It can also lead to more effective interactions with student learners (and faculty colleagues). Strategies for explaining assessment include:
- Connecting assessment to teaching and learning enhancement;

- Focusing on assuring student learning;
- Focusing on one or two aspects of a course to assess;
- Aligning assessment with scholarship of teaching and learning (SoTL).

Think about it . . .

In what ways does assessment support effective teaching?

_____

_____

_____

_____

_____

In what ways might millennial faculty align with assessment practices at your academic institution?

_____

_____

_____

_____

_____

Designing Faculty Awards and Incentives

Millennial faculty are driven by success, and acknowledgements are a way to ensure that faculty receive the recognition they deserve. Faculty awards can focus on teaching, innovation, scholarship, diversity, and service, along with more specialized—perhaps focused on areas of interest for the institution—options. At Eastern Kentucky University, the Noel Studio for Academic Creativity offers faculty several recognitions, each coming with a monetary award.

- Faculty Innovation in Teaching Award (2)
- High-Impact Practice Award (2)
- Scholarship of Teaching and Learning (1)
- Leadership (1)
- Inclusive Excellence (2)

Awards often require faculty applicants to submit documentation in a packet. Documentation includes
- Cover letter
- Letters of support (2)
- Documentation (usually focused on teaching)
- Course observations or perception of teaching

Think about it . . .

What incentives are currently in place at your academic institution?

_____

_____

_____

_____

_____

_____

How might acknowledgements support millennial faculty?

_____

_____

_____

_____

_____

_____

Considering Institutional Factors and Attributes of Successful Programs

Institutional factors always influence faculty work (scholarship, teaching, and service). Millennial faculty will benefit from an understanding of how the institution operates, what roles serve different functions, and how they might benefit from the resources offered in each area. Institutional factors such as promotion and tenure requirements, teaching loads, availability of research funding, and performance incentives such as grants and awards.

Think about it . . .

What institutional factors affect your work at your academic institution?

_____

_____

_____

_____

_____

How might millennial faculty respond to institutional factors at your institution?

_____

_____

_____

_____

_____

Brainstorm strategies for informing millennial faculty and supporting millennial faculty when navigating institutional factors at your academic institution.

_____

_____

_____

_____

_____

Building Processes and Procedures for Enhancing Infrastructure(s) for Millennial Faculty

Relationships are a priority for millennial faculty. Thus it is likely that similar values will factor in millennial faculty success. Relationships are not often considered critical within the context of faculty development programs, but they will factor in millennial faculty members' success. Institutional infrastructures can inhibit millennial faculty success but do not have to. Proper supports can be designed and implement through faculty development programs that support millennial faculty while also promoting success.

Processes that support millennial faculty should include:
- Channels for regular communication with department chair(s), dean(s), provost(s), and other academic leaders; and
- Venues for sharing input into institutional processes.

Faculty development programs can actively reduce or remove barriers—silos that often inhibit communication or collaboration. These traditional boundaries will be challenged by millennial faculty, which can result in frustrations that are counter to success. Faculty developers (or faculty development programs) can serve as set designers—ensuring that the right people, places, resources, and long-term support are in place for millennial faculty. Often, faculty development centers (or CTLs) serve as neutral (or central) resources and spaces for all faculty. They can be special—and valuable—spaces for millennial faculty, representing many of the characteristics valued already by these faculty members.

Think about it . . .

In what ways do faculty development centers—or CTLs—represent the values of millennial faculty?

_____

_____

_____

_____

_____

List barriers (or silos) at academic institutions that are unintentional that can impede millennial faculty progression and success.

_____

_____

_____

_____

_____

List obstacles at academic institutions that can be reduced through CTL involvement.

_____

_____

_____

_____

_____

The new class of faculty at your institution includes multiple millennial faculty. You are assigned to mentor a millennial. How would you go about setting priorities to ensure success as a mentor?

_____

_____

_____

_____

_____

A millennial faculty member has questions about priorities in their first year on campus. What questions would you ask? How might you help determine priorities?

_____

_____

_____

_____

_____

References

Clark, D. J., & Saulnier, B. M. (2010). Broadening the role of the teaching and learning center: From transforming faculty to transforming institutions. *Journal on Centers for Teaching and Learning, 2*, 111-130.

Kelly, R. (2009, June 30). Millennial faculty are coming: Are you ready? *Faculty Focus*. Retrieved from https://www.facultyfocus.com/articles/academic-leadership/millennial-faculty-are-coming-are-you-ready/

Kuh, G. D., Chen, D., & Laird, T. F. N. (2007). Why teacher-scholars matter: Some insights from FSSE and NSSE. *Liberal Education, 93*(4). Retrieved from https://www.aacu.org/publications-research/periodicals/why-teacher-scholars-matter-some-insights-fsse-and-nsse

Sweet, C., Blythe, H., Carpenter, R., & Cecil, T. (2018). Approaching the Holy Grail of faculty development: Evolving a CTL from a service-oriented organization to a learning-assessment unit. *Journal on Centers for Teaching and Learning, 10*, 45-58.

Tassoni, J. P. (2009). Nooks and crannies and center stages: Exploring the role of the teaching and learning center—a message from the executive editor. *Journal on Centers for Teaching and Learning, 1*, 1-6.

Waljee, J.F., Chopra, V., & Saint, S. (2018). Mentoring millennials. *JAMA, 319(*15), 1547-1548.

Millennial-Focused Faculty Development Programs Faculty Vignettes

Adult Learning Theory: A Method of Engaging Millennial Faculty

Bridget Lepore, Kean University, School of General Studies

There is extensive literature on engaging adult learners that can be useful for informing professional learning activities for students and faculty alike. When working with millennial faculty, this literature can be used as a guide to ensuring that professional development is relevant, useful, and engaging. Even better, aligning professional learning activities with adult learning theory is good for all faculty and enables faculty learning in the same type of learning environment we know works for students- one that is flexible, connected, relevant, and supportive. As a faculty member in our general education program, I have the privilege of working in a cohort that spans multiple generations and covers a variety of disciplines. Our group has a significant number of millennial faculty in it.

In working with our millennial faculty, who are bright,

dedicated, and motivated professionals, I've noticed a few common traits. Our millennial faculty are outspoken and expected to be consulted and involved in all aspects of their work lives including professional learning. Without consultation, they are less likely to accept to learning activities, especially those that they are not involved in designing. That said, when consulted, they tend to engage fully, devoting their energy and emotion to the work in front of them. They are dedicated to their teaching practice and students, often acting as passionate advocates for what is equitable, just, and inclusive. They connect quickly and share information about teaching, background, and work easily and comfortably both in person and through technology. While they may not all want to work in groups, they expect constant communication with their students and their colleagues. Like all faculty, our millennial faculty need to know what they are learning and how it will be useful to their teaching practice. They expect that learning activities are clear, concise, relevant, and easily applicable. They typically want activities that are collaborative and have immediate benefits to their work. They tend to want content-heavy activities to be delivered through technology with the ability to move through it at their own pace, on their schedule.

While the traits above are common among college and university faculty, they tend to be amplified in millennial faculty. My experience with millennial faculty while providing support, mentoring, and professional development for them—is that aligning any activities with adult learning theories such as self-directed learning, experiential earning, and transformative learning are more likely to be accepted and used. The basis of these theories is that learners need to be involved in all aspects of the process, and activities should have immediate concrete applications, increase social connection, and involve flexibility, choice, and refection. For our faculty, designing activities backwards moving from outcomes to activities while being mindful of adult learning theory has yielded learning experiences that improve teaching capacity and with it, learning for our students.

Communication, Feedback, and Sparkle: Supporting Millennial Faculty

Shanti Bruce, Nova Southeastern University, Professor/ Chair Department of Writing and Communication & Interim Chair, Department of Multidisciplinary Studies

As an administrator, I have been recruiting, hiring, and mentoring faculty for over a decade. They fill a variety of positions and range greatly in age, from 23 year olds just finishing M.A.s and newly minted Ph.D.s, to mid-and late-career professionals and those in their 70s retiring in South Florida.

In the past few years, I have noticed some differences that set millennials apart from the faculty of other generations. First, they check-in with me all the time. They ask me to review emails before they send them and copy me on almost everything. Even when we've discussed something at length, we have settled on how they will handle the situation, and I say I don't need to be copied because I am confident they can take it from here, they insist on copying me. I also get emails with subject lines that include "FOR APPROVAL," and we constantly catch up and review what they are doing and their progress. Any issue with a student also seems to escalate quickly to me, and rather than it coming from the student as in the past, the faculty member is the one who wants to bring me into the conversation.

Several years ago, I instituted individual meetings at the beginning of the academic year, so I could review with all faculty their goals/plans for teaching, service, and scholarship. This was as much to mentor and guide them as it was for me to get a chance to learn what everyone was doing. I needed these meetings because faculty weren't always forthcoming with their projects, and some of them, I just didn't often see. When our university asked each academic unit to come up with a way to improve, a millennial in our department suggested we increase these meetings and add another at the beginning of the spring semester. I was surprised at first because I thought faculty would be reluctant to give up another hour, but I realized the millennials craved this additional feedback and meet with me much more than just during these formal one-to-one meetings. These meetings are still useful as they help me maintain connections with faculty of previous generations who are used to doing their own thing, but when it is time for the millennials to have their individual meetings, I often wonder if we even need them. I am completely aware of what they are doing, and in most cases, I have already talked with them at length and helped them plan what they are doing.

Another way I have been surprised by millennials is their re-action to poor student course evaluations. A colleague of mine in another department—of a previous generation—actually refused to even go for a merit raise because he had received a single, questionable student evaluation. If he had gone for the raise, he would have been required to compile a portfolio that included, among many other items, all student evaluations. He was so bothered by the idea that someone might see the poor evaluation that he passed on the opportunity for a raise. Fast-forward several years, and both of my latest hires emailed and texted me the minute they received their first unflattering student evaluation. One asked to meet with me immediately and even included a direct link to her evaluations, so I could quickly see the critical comments. The other texted me to ask for a meeting and was near in tears when we got together. While previous colleagues hoped no one would notice a poor evaluation, the millennials brought them to my attention before I was aware of them. I carefully reviewed the evaluations with each one, analyzing what was constructive, what could be learned from them, and what parts of the evaluations might not be worth their time. On the whole, the comments weren't nearly as bad as what I had expected considering their reactions, and I spent much of our meetings trying to make them feel better, helping them to see that the comments weren't actually that bad, and sharing with them studies that have revealed bias in evaluations. Rather than sweep them under the rug, these faculty brought negative reviews straight to the department chair and wanted to spend time discussing them.

Finally, I have noticed that coffee is a big hit with millennials, just as it has been with previous generations. So much so that one put a sign on her door about coffee and another gave me a fancy bag of coffee as a gift. I guess she never noticed that I don't actually drink coffee; she just assumed it was "a thing" for everyone. In addition to providing coffee and water for the office, I started stocking La Croix in the department fridge. The level of joy and workplace satisfaction that has come with the addition of this flavored, sparkling water has far surpassed my expectations.

My takeaways in supporting millennial faculty are the need for constant communication and the craving of guidance and approval. In many ways, they are an open book, and one often says to me, "I have a 'mentor' question." She sees me as her mentor and calls me that regularly, though I have never used that word with her. Also, a little sparkle seems to go a very long way.

Millennials' Learning Preferences and the Full Value Contract: A Hospitable Recipe for Faculty Development Opportunities

Carrie Jo Coaplen, Indiana University Southeast,
Instructional Designer and Technology Consultant

Despite interacting with Millennial faculty members often, I hesitate to generalize them. However, if –as common knowledge suggests- Millennials desire flexible, collaborative, and feedback-rich professional experiences, I respectfully suggest that faculty developers can learn a lot from a traditional facilitation and a "hospitality" approach to consultations based on teams and ropes course concepts. Specifically, I refer to Project Adventure's "Full Value Contract," (FVC) which I share more about below. In mentioning "hospitality," I also imply that to build relationships with faculty (relationships being where most learning occurs), applying hospitality principles are also key to creating the aforementioned flexible, collaborative, and safe feedback-rich learning experiences. In short, as a former teams and ropes course facilitator, I believe that Millennial faculty, and most learners, will be more receptive to learning when they are warmly considered and invited into potentially challenging experiences that consider their goals, safety, and needs.

The Full Value Contract (FVC) as described in Project Adventure's canonical Adventure Based Counseling (ABC) book, *Islands of Healing* (Schoel, Prouty, & Radcliffe) asks participants, pre-activity, to agree with adherence to five general guidelines for themselves and each other. These include to (a) be present, (b) pay attention, (c) speak your truth, (d), be open to outcomes, and (e) create a safe environment. When I worked with teams, I used this model as a foundation. I also learned about the group's existing knowledge. I then guided them to set their own goals, rather than imposing my knowledge and agenda. Asking individuals about their knowledge and goals often results in more buy in and ownership of learning. Taken together, the FVC and group generated goals lead to a more purposeful, emotionally secure, and collaborative learning experience. Applied to faculty development, along with infusing the spirit of hospitality, a faculty development session can become a relationship building moment enriched with Millennials' preferences for flexibility, collaboration, and quality feedback.

Specifically, what might be considered best practices during any number of the faculty development opportunities that I am involved in that draw from the FVC and hospitality? Think about a guest who visits your home. Or imagine a ropes course participant who is 40 feet in the air on a safety wire with you at the bottom performing belay. I bet that most faculty feel as if they are either entering a strange place or hanging by a wire when they visit learning centers needing instructional support. Whether a guest, or a ropes course participant, those in our care are best served when their needs are understood and met with warmth. If we praise or offer a friendly push will depend upon an expert facilitator's ability to read the context. When I use the FVC and hospitality, faculty are more likely to learn, develop skills, and reach goals that they had a hand in creating. Millennial faculty's preferences for sensitivity to their needs, rather than academia's tendency to traditionally push our agendas, seem like a sensible and sensitive approach toward retaining as well as enriching this professional cohort.

About the Authors

Michael G. Strawser (Ph.D., University of Kentucky) is an assistant professor in the Nicholson School of Communication and Media at the University of Central Florida. Michael's research interests broadly include instructional and organizational communication. He is also the owner/lead consultant of Legacy Communication Training and Consulting, L.L.C. (www.legacyctc.com).

Russell Carpenter (Ph.D., University of Central Florida) is executive director of the Noel Studio for Academic Creativity and associate professor of English at Eastern Kentucky University. Recent books include *Studio-Based Approaches for Multimodal Projects and Writing Studio Pedagogy*. Carpenter serves as editor of the *Journal of Faculty Development*.

A special thank you to our faculty vignette contributors:

Liza Ngenye, La Sierra University
Benjamin Drury, Morton College
Aditi Paul, Pace University
Jasmin M. Goodman, Howard University
Wei Sun, Howard University
Kevin Dvorak, Nova Southeastern University
Sara L. Zeigler, Eastern Kentucky University
Anne B. Bucalos, Bellarmine University
Donna M. Elkins, Spalding University
Stephanie A. Smith, Virginia Tech
Bridget Lepore, Kean University
Shanti Bruce, Nova Southeastern University
Carrie Jo Coaplen, Indiana University Southeast

Made in the USA
Columbia, SC
13 September 2020